PERU
in Pictures

Herón Márquez

Lerner Publications Company

Contents

Website address: www.lernerbooks.com

Lerner Publications Company
A division of Lerner Publishing Group
241 First Avenue North
Minneapolis, MN 55401 U.S.A.

web enhanced @ www.vgsbooks.com

CULTURAL LIFE   46

► Religion. Language and Literature. Music and
  Dance. Art and Architecture. Modern Media.
  Sports and Recreation. Food and Drink. Holidays
  and Festivals.

THE ECONOMY   58

► Agriculture. Industry. Services. Foreign Trade.
  Illegal Economic Activities. The Future.

FOR MORE INFORMATION

Library of Congress Cataloging-in-Publication Data

Márquez, Herón.
        Peru in pictures / Heron Marquez.—Rev. and expanded.
           p.   cm. — (Visual geography series)
        Includes bibliographical references and index.
        Summary: Introduces through text and photographs the land, history, government, people, and
economy of the third largest country in South America.
        ISBN 0-8225-1999-2 (lib. bdg. : alk. paper)
        1. Peru—Juvenile literature. [1. Peru.] I. Title. II. Series: Visual geography series (Minneapolis, Minn.)
F3408.5.M355 2004
985.06'5—dc22   2003022958

Manufactured in the United States of America
1 2 3 4 5 6 - BP - 09 08 07 06 05 04

INTRODUCTION

The Republic of Peru, located on the western coast of South America, is a fascinating place. It has natural wonders, such as beaches, mountains, and jungles. Its history is filled with great civilizations, mysterious places, and a unique blend of European and Indian—also called native or indigenous—cultures. It is blessed with mineral riches and more types of plants and animals than almost any other country in the world. But Peru, which has a population of 28.4 million people, has had a difficult time benefiting from these blessings. Earthquakes, poverty, crime, political instability, and other problems have plagued the country throughout its history.

Over the centuries, native groups in Peru have produced advanced works of art, beautiful tapestries, and mysterious objects such as the Nazca desert drawings. The country was once home to the famous Inca Empire. Starting in the twelfth century, the Incas spread out from their capital of Cuzco to build an empire that ran from modern-day Ecuador to modern-day Chile. At its peak in the fifteenth century, the

Inca Empire covered roughly 300,000 square miles (777,000 square kilometers), with a population of about 16 million people. Inca civilization was noted for its extensive road system, sophisticated government, impressive architecture, and tremendous wealth.

Spanish conquerors toppled the Inca Empire in the early sixteenth century. The Spaniards, looking for gold for their king, quickly took over both Central and South America, including Peru. The Spaniards converted natives to Catholicism, the religion of Spain, and turned the natives into near slaves, forcing them to work for very little or no pay. For almost three hundred years, Peru's gold and silver were shipped off to enrich the Spanish royal family.

Peru achieved independence from Spain in the 1820s. But it still struggled politically and economically. Its new leaders fought among themselves for control. These rulers were descendants of the Spaniards. They followed Spanish customs, spoke Spanish, and practiced Catholicism. They did not change the economic system that had

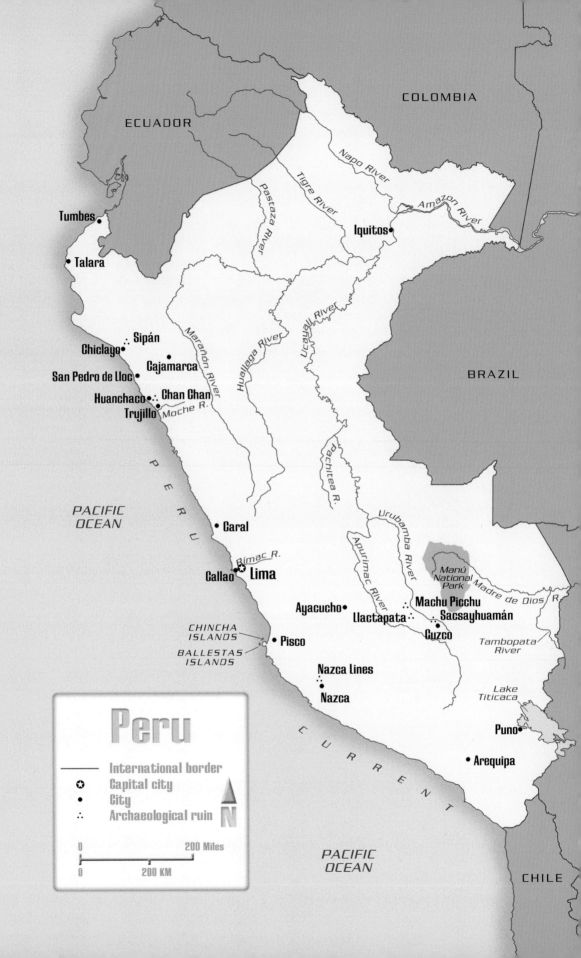

operated under Spanish rule. As a result, the Indians who lived in Peru did not benefit from the change in political power.

Throughout the twentieth century, Peruvian society was divided along racial and economic lines. Money and power rested with white people of Spanish descent, while Indians remained poor and powerless. Several times during the century, military leaders staged violent over-throws of the government. The nation also faced social problems rang-ing from widespread poverty to terrorist attacks. One of the most notorious terrorist groups is the Shining Path, based in the Peruvian countryside. Hoping to take over the government, the Shining Path carried out killings and deadly bombings in the 1980s and early 1990s. Drug traffickers also operated in the countryside, adding to the vio-lence and lawlessness. To escape the terror, thousands of rural Peruvians moved to Lima and other big cities. They crowded into run-down neighborhoods, where many lived in extreme poverty, without safe drinking water, health care, or jobs.

The situation improved for a time with the 1990 election of President Alberto Fujimori. He cracked down on terrorist groups and drug traffickers and made changes that improved Peru's economy. But Fujimori also angered Peruvians by gathering too much power into his own hands. In 2000 he was accused of election fraud and was then kicked out of office.

Finally, in July 2001, the country received a ray of hope when Alejandro Toledo Manrique was elected president. Toledo, a former shoeshine boy, had studied economics in the United States. He went on to work as a business-school professor and economist. More impor-tantly, he was an Indian—the first Indian ever elected president of Peru. Toledo began several efforts to improve life for the nation's poor, including a program to bring clean water to rural areas. By 2003, the nation's economy showed signs of improvement, and perhaps signs that Peru is headed in a new, more positive direction.

THE LAND

Peru is located on the western edge of South America. It is the third largest country on the continent. Peru borders Ecuador and Colombia on the north, Brazil to the east, Bolivia to the southeast, Chile to the south, and the Pacific Ocean on the west. Peru covers an area of 496,225 square miles (1,285,222 sq. km), slightly smaller than the state of Alaska. Its borders contain more variety of plant and animal species than almost anywhere else on earth, as well as some of the most spectacular scenery on the planet. The Andes Mountains, the second highest mountain range in the world, run through the middle of the country, dividing Peru into three distinct geographical zones.

◎ The Coast

The first zone, the coast (called the *costa* in Spanish), is a dry, desert-like strip of land that runs the entire length of the country. The coastal region runs 1,448 miles (2,330 km) along the Pacific Ocean, from

Peru's northern border with Ecuador to the southern border with Chile. The region is only about 100 miles (161 km) at its widest point. The coast region is home to Peru's capital city of Lima as well as a large portion of the country's population of 28.4 million.

Snow melting in the western slopes of the nearby mountains forms dozens of streams that flow through the coast toward the sea. But of the fifty-two streams that flow down from the mountains, only ten go all the way to the ocean. Some places along the rivers are oases—fertile, green areas in the desert. People have built towns and cities around these areas.

The Andes

The Andes Mountains comprise Peru's second major geographical zone. The Andes run the entire length of South America, forming the longest mountain chain in the world—more than 4,500 miles (7,240 km) long. The width of the Andes varies from 200 to 400 miles (322 to

644 km). The Andes are the world's second highest mountain range, after the Himalayas in southern Asia.

In Peru the highest mountain is Mount Huascarán, an extinct (no longer active) volcano, which stands 22,205 feet (6,768 meters) above sea level. Huascarán and Peru's other high peaks are covered in snow year-round. On the eastern slopes of the Andes, rainfall and melting snow form small rivers that eventually flow eastward into the Amazon, the world's second longest river.

The lower regions of the Andes have gentle slopes, wide valleys, and flat, raised areas called plateaus. People who live in the Andes make their homes in these lower regions, where most make their living as farmers. The mountain terrain is treacherous in some places. Earthquakes and landslides are common. The mountains also have deep gorges and canyons, including Colca, one of the deepest canyons in the world. At 11,333 feet (3,454 m) deep, Colca is almost twice as deep as the Grand Canyon in the United States. The rugged terrain has made it difficult for people to build roads and to travel in the mountains. Many mountain communities are isolated from each other and from the cities and the government on the coast.

The Jungle

The third major region is the jungle, called the *selva* in Spanish. The jungle covers about 60 percent of the country. The jungle starts on the eastern slopes of the Andes and descends north and east into

Colca Canyon, located in southern Peru, is one of the deepest canyons in the world.

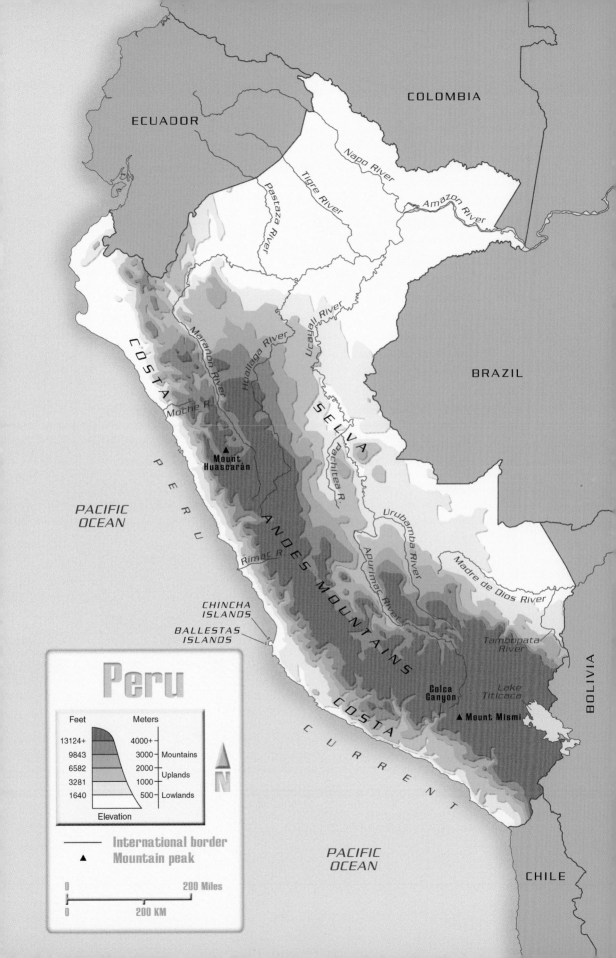

the vast basin of the Amazon River. The Peruvian jungle is a dense rain forest—a region of tall trees, high temperatures, and heavy rainfall. Little development, such as roads or big cities, has taken place there because of the dense vegetation. In addition, little of the land is usable for farming or settlement. The best way to get around the jungle is by boat or airplane.

Rivers and Lakes

Snow and heavy rainfall create many rivers in Peru, especially in the jungle. In the north and northeast, the Marañón and Ucayali rivers unite to form the Amazon—the world's biggest river by volume (the amount of water in the river). From its source in Peru, the Amazon travels eastward about 4,000 miles (6,436 km) across South America to the Atlantic Ocean. Other rivers in Peru include the Napo, Tigre, Pastaza, Pachitea, Urubamba, Madre de Dios, Tambopata, and Huallaga.

Lake Titicaca, covering about 3,200 square miles (8,288 sq. km), is the biggest lake in Peru and the second largest lake in South America. At

more than 12,500 feet (3,810 m) above sea level, it is called the world's highest navigable lake (big enough to accommodate boats). Actually, other lakes in the area are higher, but Titicaca is the highest lake with regular passenger boat service. Located in southeastern Peru, Lake Titicaca forms a border with Bolivia. More than twenty-five rivers empty into the lake, which also has forty-one islands. Many smaller lakes are scattered throughout the country.

For centuries, the source of the mighty Amazon River was a mystery. That mystery was solved in the 1970s (and reconfirmed in 2000), when researchers traced the river to the Peruvian mountains and a stream on Mount Mismi. That stream flows into the Apurimac River, which eventually flows into the Ucayali River, which flows into the Amazon.

◉ Climate

Peru's climate varies from zone to zone. Despite the adjacent Pacific Ocean, the coast is one of the driest places on earth. Annual rainfall on the coast is only 1 to 2 inches (2.5 to 5 centimeters). Most of this rain falls in winter (which occurs between May and November in Peru). Also in winter, heavy gray clouds hang over the coast. Called the *garúa*, these clouds provide moisture for crops and other plants. The Peru Current, cold ocean water traveling north from Antarctica, helps keep the area fairly cool. Temperatures in the coastal region average 60° to 65°F (16° to 18°C) in winter and 70° to 80°F (21° to 26°C) during summer.

The climate is also cool in the mountains, especially at night. In the daytime, mountain temperatures average about 55°F (13°C) year-round, warm enough for growing crops. The

The Tigre River, a tributary of the Amazon, snakes through the Peruvian rain forest. To learn more about the Amazon, go to vgsbooks.com.

El Niño–related flooding in 1998 left most of the tombs in this cemetery in Trujillo covered in mud. The flooding also caused part of the earth to collapse, exposing buried coffins *(bottom)*.

A Christmas Visitor

El Niño, which means "the child" in Spanish, takes its name from the Christ child, or Jesus Christ. Peruvian fishers made up this name because El Niño, the warm water current that affects Peru every several years, appears around Christmastime.

nights are much colder, however, with temperatures dipping below freezing, 32°F (0°C). The dry season in the mountains lasts from May to September, the rainy season from October through April. Rainfall increases farther from the coast. The western mountains sometimes receive less than 10 inches (25 cm) of rain a year, while the eastern mountains might receive more than 40 inches (102 cm) of rain each year.

The jungle has a hot, moist climate, with rain all year. The heaviest rains fall from January through April. Some areas receive as much as 103 inches (262 cm) of rain per year. The average temperature in the jungle is 75°F (24°C).

A natural phenomenon called El Niño greatly influences Peru's climate. El Niño is a current of warm water in the Pacific Ocean. About once every two to seven years, the current is particularly strong. The warm water displaces the normal cold ocean water, warming the air above it. The warm air then disrupts weather patterns in Peru, bringing heavy rains and flooding in some areas while bringing drought to others. Also during El Niño, fish supplies are reduced, because when the water warms up, fish leave their normal homes in search of colder water in other parts of the ocean.

Flora and Fauna

The Peruvian rain forest has one of the largest arrays of plant and animal species in the world, with thousands of types of birds, butterflies, and vegetation. Rain forest animals include caimans (a kind of crocodile), pumas, monkeys, macaws (a kind of parrot), storks, turtles, giant river otters, frogs, owls, jaguars, ocelots (a kind of wild cat), parrots, piranhas, and anacondas (a large snake). Flora includes mahogany and other hardwood trees, rubber trees, and epiphytes (small plants such as ferns, mosses, and orchids that grow on the trunks and branches of larger plants).

Manú National Park, a protected area in the south of Peru, is especially famous for its birds, with more than 1,000 bird species making their homes there. In fact, Manú hosts about one-tenth of all the bird species in the world. It also has more than 15,000 species of plants, 1,200 butterfly species, and 200 species of mammals.

The animal most often associated with Peru is the llama. Found in the mountains, llamas look like small camels without humps. The llama also has a head like a camel, with a large upper lip but no upper teeth. Its feet are cloven—divided in two parts. An adult llama can weigh as much as 400 pounds (182 kilograms). Although the llama moves slowly, it can leap like a deer. Since the time of the Incas, people have used llamas as pack animals—animals that carry heavy loads. People also use llama wool to make blankets and clothing, and llama meat is eaten for food. The Incas also used llama wool to make ropes. Some of these ropes were used to suspend bridges over rivers and canyons.

Alpacas and vicuñas also live in the mountains. Both animals are similar to llamas. Alpacas have fine white wool that is used to make clothing. Vicuña wool is considered the finest of all. It is extremely soft and warm. During the time of the Incas, only the Lord Inca, the top leader, was allowed to wear clothing made from vicuña wool.

The coast is home to a large number of fish and other sea animals, ranging from sea lions to squids. It also has a large number of birds. Guanays, dark birds with long necks, are found in great numbers. Their

Peruvian farmers raise **alpacas** for their soft white wool. The wool is then spun into fine cloth and used to make clothing and other textiles.

Sea lions frolic on the rocky shores of the Ballestas Islands off the coast of southeastern Peru.

droppings are used as fertilizer. The coast has few land animals because of the dry conditions, although rabbits and armadillos live there. It is also home to cacti, shrubs, and other vegetation that doesn't need much water. Grasses grow on the western slopes of the mountains. As the slopes get higher, there is more water from melting snow and the vegetation becomes more lush. Trees such as poplars and pines grow on the slopes.

Natural Resources

During Inca times, Peru was among the richest countries in the world, with a vast treasure of gold and silver. However, only a little gold remains. But the country still has great mineral wealth in the form of copper, zinc, and silver deposits. The minerals are used for exports (sales to other countries) and manufacturing. The country has oil deposits along the coast and in the jungles. The oil is used to fuel homes, cars, and businesses. Peru also has deposits of iron ore, coal, and phosphate, a rock that is used to make fertilizer.

With such a long coast, Peru also has a large supply of fish, including anchovies, sardines, and tuna. Peru is one of the world's biggest fish exporters.

The jungle has large quantities of mahogany and other hardwood trees. The wood is used for building and is exported to other countries. Peruvian farmers grow a variety of crops. Coffee, grown high in the Andes Mountains, is one of the most important. Many medicines come from the jungles of Peru. One example is aspirin, originally made from the bark of willow trees. Another is quinine, made from the bark of the cinchona tree, which is used to treat malaria. Curare, used as a muscle relaxant prior to surgery, is made from the roots and stems of the curare plant. In recent years, pharmaceutical (drug) companies have arrived in the Amazon region to harvest its medicinal plants.

Environmental Issues

Peru has a number of environmental problems, including pollution. The worst pollution is found in the cities, where factories and processing plants release pollutants into the air and water. In Lima and other cities, heavy automobile use also contributes to air pollution. In some areas, mines release mercury and other contaminants into lakes and rivers. In rural regions, farmers use chemical pesticides and fertilizers to improve their crop yields. But these chemicals can run off from farmland into rivers and streams, harming and even killing the plants and animals that live in the water.

In the rain forest, people have cut down many acres of trees—both to sell the valuable wood and to create farmland. Experts estimate that 700,000 acres (283,000 hectares) of rain forest are cleared in Peru each year. Cutting down the rain forest creates a number of environmental problems. First, without tree roots to hold the soil in place, mud can slide down hillsides and clog up rivers and streams. Cutting down the forest also destroys the homes of forest animals and plants. With the destruction of Peru's forests, species such as macaws, spectacled bears, river turtles, and sloths have become endangered—meaning that they are in danger of dying out altogether. Deforestation even affects the whole planet, because rain forests absorb carbon dioxide. Cutting the forests changes the balance of gases in the earth's atmosphere.

Rain forests at high altitudes are called cloud forests. Because the forests are so high above sea level, they are usually covered in clouds, which give the forests their name. The clouds provide water to the forest trees and plants.

To combat the problem of rain forest destruction, Peru has protected approximately 5 percent of its territory in a system of national parks, preserves, and wildlife sanctuaries. These areas are off-limits to building, logging, and other kinds of development. At 7,720 square miles (20,000 sq. km)—about half the size of Switzerland—Manú National Park is the biggest protected area in Peru. Much of the reserve has not been explored.

◉ Cities

LIMA, the capital of Peru, is the economic, cultural, and educational center of the country. It is also the largest city in Peru, with approximately 8 million people living there. Located on the Pacific Ocean and the banks of the Rímac River, the city was founded by Francisco Pizarro, a Spanish conqueror, in 1535. Pizarro originally called Lima the City of Kings.

When Spain ruled Peru, Lima was among the richest cities in the world, and it is still the richest in Peru. Factories there produce everything from textiles to food to tobacco products. Goods depart and arrive at the neighboring port of Callao. Lima boasts traditional landmarks

The sun sets in **downtown Lima.** More than 8 million people live in Lima, making it the largest and busiest city in Peru.

from the Spanish era, such as the beautiful Plaza Mayor, along with modern office buildings and businesses. The city has many restaurants, theaters, and other cultural attractions, including the National Museum of Anthropology and Archaeology.

Lima has very few tall buildings. Why? Earthquakes are frequent in Peru, and tall buildings are likely to fall down during earthquakes. So most homes in Lima are single story, and even office buildings are only a few stories tall.

TRUJILLO, with about 650,000 residents, has some of the best weather in Peru, with springlike temperatures year-round. Located on the north coast, Trujillo was founded in 1534 and named after the Spanish hometown of Francisco Pizarro. Situated in one of the most fertile valleys in Peru, Trujillo also produces a lot of agricultural products. The famous ruins of Chan Chan are located just west of the city. Created by the Chimú people around A.D. 1300, Chan Chan was once a large city with buildings made of adobe, or mud bricks.

An earthquake fault runs the length of South America, passing along the coast of Peru and right through the city of Arequipa. Over the centuries, Peru has suffered from numerous earthquakes, many of which have caused mudslides, flooding, and other destruction. A 1950 quake killed about 35,000 people in Cuzco. A quake in northern Peru killed 50,000 in 1970.

AREQUIPA The largest city in the Andes, Arequipa is known

as the White City because of the color of its buildings, which are made of sillar, a white volcanic rock. Founded in 1540, the city has a modern population of more than 600,000. It is a center for Peru's wool business and also a gateway for tourists visiting nearby Colca Canyon.

IQUITOS The largest city in Peru's jungle, Iquitos was a very rich city in the nineteenth century. Rubber trees grew in the surrounding rain forest. When demand for raw rubber grew—the rubber was used to make car tires and other products—prices went up. This created a "rubber boom" that brought great wealth to the city for several decades.

Modern Iquitos has a population of nearly 400,000. It no longer makes much money from the rubber business, however. Instead, the city hosts tourists who arrive there to start journeys into the Amazon River basin. The city is also a center for the buying and selling of fish, fruits, and herbal medicines. But it can be reached only by air or water, because there are no roads into the city—the thick jungle makes it nearly impossible to build roads there. Because of heavy rainfall and flooding, some city dwellers build their houses on stilts.

 Visit vgsbooks.com, where you'll find links to more information about Peru's cities. Discover what there is to see and do, what the climate and weather are like, learn about population statistics, and more.

CUZCO Located in the southern Andes, Cuzco was the original capital of the Inca Empire. In the Inca language, *cuzco* means "navel." The name was meant to signify that Cuzco was the center, or navel, of the universe. The oldest continuously populated city in South America, Cuzco was founded in the twelfth century. It has a modern population of about 300,000 people.

The city appeals to people who are interested in archaeology because it is close to Machu Picchu, famous Inca ruins. Cuzco also contains the Inca Temple of the Sun and parts of a wall that surrounded the city in Inca times. Cuzco was once a Spanish government center, with many colonial (Spanish-era) buildings constructed atop old Inca walls. Many people in modern Cuzco work in the tourist industry, catering to travelers who come to visit Machu Picchu and other Inca-era sites. Other city industries are textile manufacturing, brewing, sugar refining, and chocolate production.

HISTORY AND GOVERNMENT

Humans have lived in Peru for at least ten thousand years and perhaps as long as twenty thousand years. Some historians think that the ancestors of Peru's early residents wandered south along the Pacific coast from Alaska, after crossing a land bridge that once linked North America to Asia. But new evidence suggests that Peru's first inhabitants might have come from other parts of the world.

Peru's early inhabitants settled along the coast and lived by hunting animals and gathering plants for food. The earliest villages in Peru were built about 2500 B.C. Villagers wove cotton, fished, and grew such crops as beans, corn, and potatoes. By about 1800 B.C., people had also established villages in the surrounding hills and mountains. By about 1300 B.C., they had started using irrigation, a system of diverting water to crops.

◉ Early Civilizations

Early Peru was home to a number of native groups. The most notable were the Chavín, who lived about 800 B.C. in the north-central mountains. The Chavín dominated the region for about five hundred years. Through their arts and religion, the Chavín influenced cultures that came after them, including the Paracas, who lived south of present-day Lima. The Paracas, flourishing from about 600 to 175 B.C., were skilled in weaving. Their textiles are considered the best of pre-Columbian times (the era before the Spanish arrival). The Paracas also mummified, or preserved, the bodies of their dead.

About 100 B.C., the Nazca culture emerged in Peru. The Nazca made ceramics, as well as huge, mysterious lines on the land of their desert territory. The Nazca Lines form patterns, spirals, and animal figures that go on for miles. No one is absolutely sure why they were made or what purpose they served. Adding to the mystery: the complete images are only visible from the sky.

The Moche, situated around Trujillo, emerged about A.D. 100. They ruled along the coast around the Moche River valley. The Moche created great temple-pyramids, made of millions of mud bricks. They also

The **Sipán archaeological site** near Chiclayo contains many rich treasures. Scientists have been excavating the tombs there since the 1980s.

created irrigation systems and advanced metalwork. Grave robbers discovered one of their burial tombs in 1986 near the town of Sipán. The tomb contained the skeleton of a Moche ruler called the Lord of Sipán. The site, which dates from about A.D. 300, provided rich treasure. The skeleton was surrounded by gold, silver, and ceramic items.

The Wari were the next great civilization. They flourished from about A.D. 600 to 850 in the valleys of central Peru. The Wari were the first people in Peru to aggressively take over other cultures. They were probably the first to create an empire—a centralized government with control over different regions. Wari culture disappeared almost as fast as it appeared, but historians do not know why.

After the Wari, the Tiahuanaco culture emerged. This culture was a coalition of various regional kingdoms. The best known of these kingdoms was the Chimú culture, which flourished around the eleventh century. The Chimú built large cities. Among them was Chan Chan, with buildings made entirely of mud bricks. The city was possibly the largest in South America in its time and might have been home to as many as 100,000 people. The modern-day Aymara people, who make their homes around Lake Titicaca, are descendants of Tiahuanaco peoples.

Caral, in central Peru, is thought to be the oldest city in the Americas. It is believed to date from around 2600 B.C.

◉ The Incas

The Incas appeared sometime before 1200, settling around Cuzco in the Andes Mountains. Inca legend has it that the Sun God created their first leader, Manco Cápac, along with his sister. The Sun God told Manco Cápac and his sister to build a city at the center of the universe. They would know this place, the Sun God said, because the land would be so fertile that a golden staff thrown into the ground would disappear into the rich earth. Legend says that the brother and sister threw down their staff at Cuzco.

The Incas were ruled by a king called the Lord Inca, considered to be a god by his subjects. He owned everything in the empire, from the land to the people to the crops. The Incas were great builders, planners, and administrators, skills they used to create a very sophisticated society. They built their empire by conquering neighboring tribes. The conquered people were allowed to govern local areas, but they had to take orders from the Lord Inca.

The Incas also used a system of forced labor called the *mita*. Under this system, the king provided housing and food for the people. In exchange, the people were assigned jobs, such as farming, bridge building, and road building. In this way, the Incas built a road system that extended all over the empire. A road along the coast was 2,520 miles (4,054 km) long, and one through the Andes was 3,250 miles (5,229 km) long. The Incas also built thousands of miles of smaller roads connecting to the main roads. Some roads were dirt, while others were paved with flat stones.

The Incas did not know about the wheel, so they did not have carts or carriages. Instead, people traveled the roads by foot, often with animals carrying cargo. Runners traveled the roads, carrying messages for the Lord Inca. Along the roadsides, the Incas built thousands of stone buildings to house runners, government officials, and animals.

The Incas kept records of local populations, crop yields, and other statistics using the quipu, an accounting device made of a series of knotted, color-coded strings. The knots and colors indicated different items and numbers. The Incas also had an elaborate agricultural system. By digging terraces (flat fields cut into mountainsides), they were able to expand the amount of land that could be used to grow crops. They also used irrigation canals and ditches to bring water to their crops. In this way, the Incas grew enough food to feed their people, with some left over for times when crop yields were poor.

In the early fifteenth century, a leader named Pachacuti Inca Yupanqui accelerated expansion of the empire. By the mid-fifteenth century, the Incas had established one of the greatest and richest empires in the world. They had a great deal of gold and silver. Their empire covered about 300,000 square miles (777,000 sq. km), with a population of 9 to 16 million. The territory included most of modern-day Peru and Ecuador and parts of Bolivia, Chile, Argentina, and Colombia. By the start of the sixteenth century, the Incas had built many great cities, including Machu Picchu near Cuzco.

In about 1527, a Lord Inca named Huayna Cápac died, and his empire was divided between his sons, Atahualpa and Huáscar. Atahualpa was given the northern half of the empire. He based his kingdom in Quito, where he had been born. Huáscar was given Cuzco and the southern half of the empire. The brothers were not satisfied with the arrangement, however. They went to war to see who would control the whole territory. By 1530 Atahualpa had defeated Huáscar. The struggle greatly weakened the empire. The Incas were still recovering from the civil war when a new threat arrived at the city of Tumbes in 1532—an army of Spanish conquistadors, or conquerors, consisting of 180 men and horses.

To discover more about the Inca's fascinating civilization, historical facts about Peru, a biography on Francisco Pizarro, and government information, go to vgsbooks.com for links.

The Spanish Empire

The small Spanish force was led by Francisco Pizarro, who, from his base in Panama City to the north, had heard about the fabulous wealth of the Incas. Atahualpa, curious about the newcomers and confident of the strength of his army, agreed to meet the Spaniards in a friendly meeting at Cajamarca. But the Spaniards betrayed the Indians, killed hundreds of them, and captured Atahualpa. The Spaniards held him for months, demanding a ransom of tons of gold for his release. Although the Indians paid the ransom, in the spring of 1533 Pizarro had Atahualpa killed anyway.

In the summer of 1533, another Spanish force arrived, five hundred men strong, along with thousands of Indians who had been conquered earlier by the Incas and wanted revenge. The Spaniards fought with horses, guns, cannons, and armor against Inca warriors armed with only clubs, spears, arrows, and slings. The Spanish conquered Cuzco within a year.

With Cuzco's defeat, the Inca Empire fell into chaos. Despite occasional rebellions by indigenous peoples, Peru (and other parts of South

This drawing shows Atahualpa being captured by the Spaniards. During his quest to conquer Peru in 1533, Pizarro had many Inca put to death.

America) became a Spanish colony—a region controlled by Spain. The Spanish set up an administrative system called the *encomienda* to run their new territory. Under this system, the Spanish king gave tracts of Peruvian land to loyal Spanish settlers. The settler not only got the land but also Indians to work it (sometimes local Indians and sometimes people brought in from other parts of the country). The Indians were also forced to work in Spanish-owned mines and mills. In addition, they had to pay tribute to the Spanish conquerors in the form of gold, silver, crops, eggs, salt, game, and other goods.

In 1535 Pizarro ordered that a new capital be built on the Pacific coast at the Rímac River. Pizarro called it the City of Kings, but it eventually came to be known as Lima (named for either the river or a yellow flower that grew near the city). The Spaniards also gave the entire region a new name—Peru—from an Indian word meaning "land of abundance."

The conquest of Peru made Pizarro and his men rich, but they were soon fighting among themselves. Pizarro arrested and killed his second in command, Diego de Almagro, and in turn was killed by Almagro's followers in 1541. Despite the fighting, by 1542 Lima was one of the wealthiest cities in the world. It became the center of Spanish rule for almost all of South America. The Spanish built palaces, churches, universities, and grand homes in the city.

As the Spaniards took firm control of the country, they sought to erase traces of the Inca Empire by building churches and other official buildings over former Inca temples and other structures. The new rulers did not hesitate to move all the people from a native village if the land was needed for something else. Combined with the encomienda system, this forced relocation led to the destruction of many Indians, who died from starvation, overwork, and abuse. Millions of Indians also died from diseases such as smallpox and measles, which the Spaniards had brought from Europe. (The Indians had never before been exposed to these diseases and had no natural resistance to them.) Short on labor, the Spanish imported shiploads of slaves from Africa to work on farms and in mines.

The surviving Indians periodically rebelled against the Spanish without success. The rebellions ended in 1572, when the Spanish captured and killed Túpac Amaru, who claimed to be the last Inca ruler. The power of colonial Peru grew during the seventeenth century, as the mining of silver and gold increased. Lima became the religious, economic, and cultural center of South America. More immigrants arrived from Spain to seek wealth, and the Spanish government continued to give land, leadership positions, and Indian laborers to the newcomers.

Settlers from Spain formed the political and business elite and maintained control of the country for generations. But by the eighteenth century, the ethnic mixture of Peru was changing. Along with European-born Spaniards were many Spaniards who had been born in Peru. These people were called criollos. Some Spaniards married Indians and had

A Peruvian man holds a **portrait of Túpac Amaru.** Amaru claimed he was the last Inca ruler. He led his people in a rebellion against the Spaniards, hoping to win freedom from their rule. Amaru was captured and killed in 1572.

mixed-race children, called mestizos. Black slaves also intermarried with Europeans and Indians, further expanding the nation's racial mix.

By the start of the nineteenth century, the criollos and mestizos far outnumbered European-born Spaniards. But criollos were treated as second-class citizens, and mestizos were discriminated against because of their Indian heritage. In Peru and other South American countries, criollos and mestizos grew resentful of Spanish control. What's more, Spanish rulers continued to ship the country's gold and silver back to Spain, leaving little wealth for the local people. More and more, Peruvians thought of Peru, not Spain, as their homeland. The discontent grew, finally erupting in a war for independence.

Independence

By 1820, despite growing opposition to Spanish rule, many people in Lima were still loyal to Spain. Spain also kept 25,000 troops near the capital, so it was hard for revolts to start inside the country. But two generals from neighboring countries began pressuring the Spanish. José de San Martín and Simón Bolívar had already helped liberate Chile, Ecuador, Venezuela, and Bolivia from Spain. San Martín entered Peru in 1820 with 4,500 men. He took over Lima and declared Peru's independence on July 28, 1821. After meeting with San Martín at Guayaquil, Ecuador, Bolívar agreed to finish the fighting. The fight went on until 1824, when Bolívar's army finally defeated the Spaniards at the Battles of Junín and Ayacucho. The battles marked the end of Spanish control in South America. Bolívar became the first president of Peru, and the country's first constitution was enacted in 1827.

Simón Bolívar

The new government did not benefit Peru's Indians in any way. Although the encomienda system had by then been abolished, Indians still performed backbreaking labor in Spanish-owned mines and on Spanish-owned farms. They still had to pay tribute to Spanish landowners. Some blacks remained legally enslaved. Power and legal rights were still concentrated with white landowners.

The political system was chaotic. In the late 1820s and early 1830s, various military leaders fought several civil wars for control of the country. The fighting so weakened Peru that Bolivia took over Lima in 1835 and forced the two countries to merge. The merger led to war in 1836 with neighboring Chile, which was afraid of the power of the combined countries. When Chile won the war in 1839, Peru and Bolivia separated.

The war with Chile weakened Peru's economy. The nation also suffered from government corruption: officials took bribes and stole from the government treasury. In 1840 the country's fortunes began to turn around, however. Peru's Chincha Islands, northwest of Pisco, were found to have extensive deposits of guano, or bird droppings. The guano was a great source of fertilizer, used for growing crops. European merchants bought large amounts of guano, and the "guano boom," as it was known, contributed a lot of money to Peru's economy. New immigrants arrived in Peru, specifically laborers from China and Japan. They took jobs on cotton and sugar plantations and helped build railroad lines over the Andes.

> Guano was so valuable during the guano boom that in 1853 and 1854, Peru's president and one of his generals fought one another for control of the Chincha Islands. The conflict was called the Guano War.

The political situation also improved when General Ramón Castilla was elected president. He served from 1845 to 1851 and again from 1855 to 1862. He tried to end government corruption, and his leadership stabilized the country. He abolished slavery and the requirement that natives pay tribute to Spanish landowners. He also strengthened Peru's army and navy and developed a new constitution, enacted in 1860.

Once Castilla left power, the country again was thrown into turmoil. The guano boom, which had accounted for about 80 percent of Peru's exports at its height, came to an end. Government corruption again became a major problem. Then Spain tried to regain control in Peru, taking over the Chincha Islands in 1864. But Chile, Bolivia, and Ecuador helped Peru defeat the Spanish in 1866. Peru signed a truce with Spain in 1871.

Peru then turned to focusing on developing its economy. The country expanded its roads, bridges, and railroad system into the mountains. This transportation network helped the government spread its influence and helped improve the economy in the countryside. But the building programs proved costly, and the country had to borrow money from foreign countries to pay its bills. President Manuel Pardo enacted a series of economic reforms shortly after taking office in 1872. Pardo, a banker and the first nonmilitary ruler of Peru, cut spending in just about every government department and reduced the size of the army.

In 1873 Pardo entered into an alliance with Bolivia, which again raised fears in Chile and led to another war with Chile in 1879. The conflict, known as the War of the Pacific (1879–1883), proved disastrous for

As a result of **Manuel Pardo's** alliance with Bolivia, Peru was once again at odds with Chile. The two nations fought the War of the Pacific for four long years.

Peru. Chile defeated the two allies, and its soldiers took over Lima. After four years of war, Peru was forced to give up valuable land on its southern border with Chile.

The war left Peru almost bankrupt, forcing it to seek funds from international bankers and industrialists, specifically from Great Britain and the United States. In exchange for money, the lenders wanted greater influence over Peru's internal affairs. The foreign bankers and industrialists took control of the country's remaining guano deposits, railroads, and other holdings. In some ways, Peru was once again a colony of a foreign power. The Indians, meanwhile, suffered greatly no matter who owned the land and businesses. They still labored under harsh conditions for meager pay. They did not enjoy the same rights as white Peruvians, such as the right to vote.

One of the few bright spots during this time was a boom in rubber prices, providing income that greatly helped Peru. With vast rubber-tree holdings, the area around Iquitos especially benefited. But the boom ended after only a few decades, as buyers found cheaper sources of rubber in Southeast Asia.

A sense of order returned to Peru under the leadership of General Andrés Avelino Cáceres, who held office during much of the 1890s. He helped stimulate Peru's economy, but he did so by allowing foreign businesses to operate in Peru. In this way, outsiders took control of major Peruvian industries, such as oil, sugar, and textiles.

A New Century

The early twentieth century was a period of relative peace and prosperity for Peru. The country modernized, with new transportation, communications, and business systems. The sugar, cotton, and mining markets picked up. As Peru became more industrialized, people left the countryside for jobs in the cities.

One of the architects of this modernization was Augusto Leguía y Salcedo, who served as president legally from 1908 to 1912. After leaving office, he convinced the military to help him take over the government illegally in 1919. He wrote a new constitution in 1920 and made educational and social reforms that helped the poor. But he also ruled as a dictator—a ruler with absolute power. He imprisoned political opponents and attacked groups that opposed him, such as labor unions and newspapers. He borrowed a lot of money, putting the country in a great deal of debt. The military finally kicked him out of office in 1930. He was imprisoned and charged with stealing government funds.

A reformer named Víctor Raúl Haya de la Torre had created a new political party, the American Popular Revolutionary Alliance (APRA), in 1924. The group called for radical reforms in Peru. It sought more rights for workers, better treatment of Indians, and a distribution of wealth to help the poor. The Leguía government had had the party banned.

But Haya de la Torre, a brilliant speaker, gathered a lot of support for his cause. The 1930s in Peru were marked by violent battles between liberals (leftists) such as Haya de la Torre and conservatives (rightists), who controlled the government. Several political leaders were assassinated, and the nation's richest families called on the military to protect their property and power. In 1932 APRA supporters took over Trujillo and demanded changes from the government. The army took back the city, killing hundreds of APRA members.

The ban on APRA was dropped in the mid-1940s, and the party was allowed to participate in elections. In 1945 APRA-backed candidate José Luis Bustamante y Rivero, a liberal lawyer, won the presidential election. But he then broke with APRA over the party's part in political violence,

including the killing of a newspaper editor and a naval mutiny. The resulting turmoil led the military to again take over the government. In 1948 it installed General Manuel Odría as the nation's new leader.

Odría cracked down on APRA. He instituted capitalistic economic policies—policies that favored private business—but he also improved relations with labor unions and the poor. He created charity and other social assistance programs. Manufacturing and exports increased. Despite how he had come to power, Odría was able to usher in some much needed economic prosperity for the country.

Civilian rule finally returned in 1963 when Fernando Belaúnde Terry, an architect and urban planner, was elected president. Belaúnde Terry, a moderate politician, opened up the interior of the country by constructing a major highway through the Andes. He also built new schools, including universities. But his term in office was plagued by budget shortfalls, inflation (rising prices), and growing social unrest. Especially in the mountains, leftist rebels—people who championed the rights of the poor over big business—began to fight with the government and take over lands.

In 1968, with rebels operating in the Andes, the military again took over the government, installing General Juan Velasco Alvarado as president. Velasco was a mestizo. He had grown up poor, going to school barefoot because his parents couldn't afford to buy him shoes. He proved to be a reformer. Even though he suspended the constitution and became a dictator, he also instituted land reform. His government took over private estates and turned them into cooperatives, farms that were owned and operated by the peasants who worked there. The government also took over foreign-owned banks, oil businesses, mines, and utility companies (such as electric and telephone companies). Employees were given more say in the running of the companies where they worked.

Indian people gained more rights, although they still suffered from poverty and discrimination.

Velasco ran into problems with labor unions, businesspeople, and some members of the military, however, because his policies took power away from them. Already in bad health, Velasco was forced to leave office in 1975. A new group of military men took over the government. Their leader was General Francisco Morales Bermúdez, a more conservative man who did away with some of Velasco's changes. Morales Bermúdez served only a few years and spent much of his time fighting severe inflation, a trend that crippled the economy. Military rule soon proved unpopular and civilian rule returned in 1980, when Belaúnde Terry was again elected president.

Though popular, Belaúnde Terry also ran into trouble. The country encountered an economic downturn, a growing debt crisis, and more hyperinflation. Social conditions declined in Peru. Life expectancy rates decreased, while malnutrition, unemployment, and infant deaths increased.

The problems got so bad that leftist groups again tried to overthrow the government. The Shining Path—a violent Communist group that believed in a state-run economy with no private property—found many new members, especially in mountain areas, where people were the poorest and most desperate. The Shining Path used terrorist tactics such as bombings and executions of civilians, soldiers, and government officials. By the time Belaúnde Terry left office in 1985, about six thousand people had died at the hands of rebels and government-backed anti-rebel groups. To escape the terror, tens of thousands of peasants left the countryside for Lima and other big cities.

Things got even worse under Belaúnde Terry's successor, Alan García Pérez, a member of APRA. García, at thirty-six the youngest president in Peru's history, was popular at first. He tried to deal with the country's economic crisis by increased government intervention. His government nationalized, or took control of, privately owned banks. But his popularity dropped as the economic crisis continued.

Adding to García's troubles, by 1985 Peru was experiencing a huge drug-trafficking problem. More and more poor people were growing and

processing coca plants to make cocaine, an illegal drug that brought high prices in foreign countries. As the army sought to end the drug trade by burning coca fields, the coca growers paid Shining Path rebels to protect their operations, increasing the death and violence. Thousands more people were killed.

Peru was at its lowest point when the 1990 presidential elections took place. More than three thousand people were killed in political fighting that year alone. The economy was in ruins. Shortages of food, water, and electricity were common. Corruption scandals involving García's government erupted, further angering citizens.

Voters were ready for a change. At first, it seemed that a popular author, Mario Vargas Llosa, might win the presidential election. But a little-known agronomist (agricultural manager) named Alberto Fujimori defeated Vargas Llosa for the presidency. Fujimori, part of the Change '90 Party, called for tough measures against rebel groups and tighter controls on the economy. By 1992 Fujimori had suspended the constitution, arguing that he needed to curtail people's rights in order to fight rebels, drug dealers, government corruption, and inflation.

The economy started growing at a healthy rate, and inflation dropped dramatically. Fujimori arrested Shining Path and other rebel leaders. He was hailed as a hero. But once the situation improved, Fujimori did not give up the extra power he had gained by suspending the constitution. In fact, he created a new constitution that gave him even more power, allowing him to run for another term in office. He was easily reelected in 1995, and his party won a large majority in the new congress.

People soon started grumbling because Fujimori began acting more and more like a dictator than an elected leader, ignoring other people in his party and cracking down on opponents. He oversaw the sale of

This photograph, taken in 1984 near Ayacucho, Peru, is the first known photograph of the rebel group known as the **Shining Path.**

THE JAPANESE IN PERU

Although most people in Peru are Indian, Spanish, or a combination of both, Peru is also home to a number of Asians. Japanese and Chinese immigrants arrived in Peru in the 1850s to take jobs building railroads and doing farmwork.

During World War II (1939–1945), the United States persecuted Americans of Japanese descent (Japan was a U.S. enemy during the war), and Peru did the same. The Peruvian government, an ally of the United States, passed a law restricting the freedoms of Japanese people in Peru. The Peruvian government took away their businesses, closed their schools, and arrested many of them without charges.

In the decades after the war, Japanese people gained higher status in Peruvian society. In 1990 Alberto Fujimori *(above)*, the son of Japanese immigrants who had lost their business because of government actions in World War II, was elected president of Peru.

government industries to private businesses, a policy that attracted much opposition, which in turn weakened the economy. In 1998 El Niño hit Peru. It caused widespread flooding, landslides, and deaths, further weakening the economy. As the economy began to recover in 2000, Fujimori announced that he was seeking another term in office.

The announcement was met with much criticism inside and outside Peru. Alejandro Toledo, an Indian, economist, and a business-school professor, was among those who challenged Fujimori for office. Another candidate was former president Alan García. During the course of the election, Fujimori was accused of election fraud, and the Peruvian congress kicked him out of office. He left the country and became a citizen of Japan.

After defeating García in a runoff election, Toledo became president in June 2001. A former shoeshine boy, Toledo was the first Indian in Peru's history to be elected president. In September the Peruvian government asked Japan to arrest Fujimori. They accused him of being involved in the murder and disappearance of twenty-five people killed by military death squads in the 1990s. Japan refused to arrest him, and two years later, Peru asked Japan to hand over Fujimori so he could stand trial in Lima. Japan again refused the request because Japanese law protects its own citizens from facing trial in other countries, and Japan

Peru's first Indian president, Alejandro Toledo took office on July 28, 2001. He has vowed to end poverty and uphold democratic ideals. Learn more about Toledo and the Peruvian government at vgsbooks.com.

and Peru do not have any extradition treaties. The Peruvian government continues to uncover charges against Fujimori and to issue new international arrest warrants.

As president, Toledo has successfully obtained a $50 million loan from the World Bank, an international lending organization, to develop social programs, such as water and sanitation projects. Under his leadership, the Peruvian economy shows signs of improving.

Government

Peru has a republican system of government, in which the people elect their leaders. The constitution, rewritten several times since independence, was most recently ratified in 1993. According to this constitution, voting is mandatory for everyone between the ages of eighteen and seventy. Those who fail to vote could face fines.

The chief executive and head of state is the president, who is elected by citizens to a five-year term. The legislature consists of a unicameral (one-house) congress with 120 members. The congressional members are also elected to five-year terms. The highest judicial authority is the supreme court, with lower courts handling civil and criminal cases. For local governance, Peru is divided into twenty-five administrative regions. Voters elect regional presidents and other leaders.

THE PEOPLE

Peru is home to 28.4 million people. The population is growing at a rate of about 1.6 percent per year. At that growth rate, Peru's population is expected to reach 43 million by 2050. Peru's government would like to see the growth rate slow, since it is difficult to produce enough food to feed everyone. It is also difficult to provide clean water and sanitation services for so many people.

Peru's population density is low, however, with only 59 people per square mile (23 people per sq. km). But this figure is misleading, since the mountains and jungle are sparsely populated and more than two-thirds of Peru's people are crowded into the big cities. In fact, some parts of the Lima-Callao metropolitan area are home to several thousand people per square mile. Since terrorism has disrupted life in the countryside, more and more people, especially the native poor, have made their way to Lima and other big cities. About 72 percent of Peru's people live in cities.

Ethnic Mixture

The mix of people who live in Peru reflects the country's torturous history. Before the invasion by Spaniards, Indians made up the entire population of present-day Peru. Their numbers have been greatly reduced over the centuries, through disease, overwork, and poverty, yet the native people still make up the largest percentage of the country's population—about 45 percent. The largest indigenous groups are the Quechuas, descendants of the Incas, and the Aymaras.

Most Indian peoples live in mountain areas, although many have also moved to the cities in search of work. An estimated 250,000 Indians, representing about fifty small tribes, still live in the jungles of the Amazon basin. Among the best known of these tribes are the Yaguas, Jívaros, and Machiguengas. Some Peruvian jungles are so remote that the native peoples there have rarely, if ever, seen Europeans or other nonnatives. It is hard to build infrastructure such as water systems or roads in the dense jungles and high mountains, so

This **Quechua Indian girl** is wearing traditional clothing. The Quechua Indians, descendants of the Incas, are the largest indigenous group in Peru.

many Indians live much as their ancestors did, raising livestock and growing crops with simple hand tools and fishing in lakes and rivers. Despite the election of Alejandro Toledo, the country's Indian population continues to live difficult lives at the lowest levels of society.

Mestizos make up about 37 percent of the population, while white people of Spanish descent make up about 15 percent. Spanish-descended whites, whose ancestors took over the country in the sixteenth century, continue to be the most powerful people in Peru—holding the highest positions in business and government. Mestizos tend to be middle class, while the Indians are the poorest. The remainder of Peru's population is made up mostly of small numbers of people of Japanese, Chinese, and African heritage.

Social Services

Given the poverty and political turmoil in the country, it is not surprising that life is tough in Peru. According to U.S. government estimates, about 50 percent of Peru's people live below the poverty line. About 9.4 percent of adults are unemployed. About half of Peru's school-age children are malnourished. For many people, daily life means doing whatever is necessary to stay alive—working at any available job for very low pay. Because of its economic troubles, the government has not been able to provide good social services, such as health care or welfare, to its people.

The country's major cities, especially Lima, are overcrowded with rural people who have come to the cities looking for a better life. Large areas of the capital are filled with shantytowns—groups of houses made of wooden boards, cardboard, and sheet metal that people erect almost overnight. Life in rural Peru is also difficult, with few schools, doctors, medical clinics, or sanitation services available.

Shantytowns such as this one are scattered throughout the nation's large cities, especially Lima. Most shantytowns do not have running water, sanitation services, or electricity.

Despite these hardships, Peru does have a few programs to care for disadvantaged people. The government provides payments to people who suffer from illness or disabilities. Peru also has a system to pay unemployed people while they look for work. A pension law, passed in 1974, provides for monthly payments to retired people.

Health Care

Health care in Peru lags far behind that of many other nations. Peru has only an estimated 93 doctors and 115 nurses for every 100,000 people. (The United States, by contrast, has approximately 279 doctors and 972 nurses for every 100,000 people.) Many Peruvians, especially in rural areas, rely on *curanderos*, traditional healers who use plants, prayers, and rituals to cure illness.

The infant mortality, or death, rate in Peru—37 deaths per every 1,000 births—is quite high. By contrast, the United States has only 6.75 deaths per 1,000 births. Life expectancy is 68 years for Peruvian men and 73 years for Peruvian women.

People setting up shanties (homes) in Peru's cities generally build them on public lands, then they wait for the government to give them ownership of the property and to set up basic water and electrical services. This process can sometimes take years, during which time people live in squalid conditions. But, eventually, some shantytowns become decent areas, with substantial homes and shops.

SACRED BUT DANGEROUS

Peruvians have grown coca plants and chewed their leaves for more than four thousand years. The Incas considered the plant to be sacred. Only nobles and priests were allowed to chew it. When chewed, the leaves produce a slight narcotic, or druglike, effect in the user. Chewing the leaves also improves endurance and reduces hunger and fatigue. Chewing coca plants is still common in Peru, especially among miners.

But coca plants are also the basis for cocaine, a powerful illegal drug. Many Peruvian growers have begun to grow coca on large plantations. The coca is then made into cocaine and shipped to the United States and other nations. The Peruvian government has tried to crack down on the illegal cocaine trade. It tries to put coca growers out of business by burning their plants.

Much of the country's water is not safe for drinking because Peru lacks adequate water treatment plants and sewer facilities. Many water supplies are polluted with human and industrial wastes. Only about 25 percent of city residents and 10 percent of rural residents have safe water sources. This situation has created a health risk. Many people get sick with cholera and other diseases from drinking the contaminated water. This situation is worst in rural areas and in the shantytowns of Lima and other cities.

AIDS (acquired immunodeficiency syndrome), a worldwide health epidemic, has affected Peru as well. The United Nations estimates that more than 71,000 Peruvian adults are living with either AIDS or HIV, the virus that causes the disease. About 4,600 people have died from AIDS in Peru. Still, health officials classify the epidemic level in Peru as low. Less than 1 percent of the adult population is infected with HIV, compared to some African nations with HIV-infection rates of 20 percent or higher. Most infected people in Peru are homosexual men and prostitutes, but health officials fear that the virus is spreading to the general population. The Peruvian government and some private groups have started AIDS education programs, including teaching people about condoms, which help control the sexual spread of HIV.

Education and Child Labor

Because Peru is poor, the government has had a hard time paying teachers and building schools. As a result, its educational system is poor, and many people are illiterate—unable to read or write. During times of political unrest, schools have been disrupted or shut down.

In the early 1970s, the nation's overall literacy rate (percentage of people who could read and write) was 75 percent. In rural areas, the literacy rate was less than 50 percent. Although the overall literacy rate has improved to about 90 percent, literacy is still low in rural areas. Rates are also lower for females than males—86 percent compared to 95 percent, respectively. Peruvian girls are generally expected to stay home to help with housework and the care of younger siblings instead of going to school.

The Peruvian government provides free public education for children. In 1968 the government instituted a three-level school system. The first level is kindergarten. The second level is primary school, and the third level is secondary school (junior high and high school). About 88 percent of primary-school-age children are enrolled in primary school. Most classes are taught in Spanish, but some schools teach classes in the Quechua or Aymara language. Although primary-school enrollment is fairly high, many Peruvian children do not attend secondary school, or they drop out before graduation.

Many children drop out because they need to work to help support their families. Experts report that approximately 44 percent of Peruvian children ages 15 to 19, and more than 5 percent of children ages 10 to 14, hold jobs of some kind. Many young people work on

Many **primary schoolchildren** in Peru wear uniforms. These children attend school in San Pedro de Lloc.

farms or in factories, gold mines, or stone quarries. The work is often dangerous. The Peruvian government has passed laws meant to restrict child labor. Yet many children work in illegal industries or in businesses that are unregulated by the government, so child labor laws are difficult to enforce.

Most Peruvians do not attend university, due to poverty and a lack of preparatory education. Still, Peru has twenty-five national universities and ten private universities, with a student population of more than 350,000. The leading universities are located in Lima, Arequipa, Trujillo, and Cuzco. The National Autonomous University of San Marcos, opened in Lima in 1551, was the first university in the Americas.

Visit vgsbooks.com for links to websites with additional information about the people of Peru, including Peruvian indigenous groups such as the Tiahuanaco peoples, the Aymaras, and many others.

Women in Peru

Traditionally, women in Peru were subservient to men. Few women attended school or worked outside the home. Women were expected to care for their husbands and children. Women often suffered violence and other abuse at the hands of their husbands. In the Peruvian countryside, many of these attitudes and inequalities persist.

In the cities, trends have begun to change. Women in shantytowns have organized among themselves to improve life for their families. In urban areas, almost as many women as men attend college, and women have started entering into professions such as banking, teaching, and law. Women hold about 10 percent of the 120 seats in Peru's congress.

About 69 percent of married women in Peru use birth control, although educated and upper-class women are more likely to use birth control than poor women. The typical Peruvian woman has about three children in her lifetime. Abortion is illegal in Peru, except when the mother's life is in danger.

Urban and Rural Life

Daily life varies widely in Peru, depending on income, location, and ethnic background. Some urban dwellers, particularly the white and mestizo middle and upper classes, live much like people in the United States and other industrialized nations. They buy name-brand products at shopping malls, drive cars, live in comfortable homes and apartments, and wear Western-style clothing such as business suits, blue jeans, and tennis shoes. City dwellers work in factories, government offices, banks, and other businesses.

However, a large portion of urban dwellers, particularly those in the shantytowns of Lima, live a destitute existence in makeshift houses without electricity, water, or sanitation. Many shantytown dwellers arrived from the countryside in the late twentieth century. They hoped to find employment in the city, but for many, their hopes have not been fulfilled. Lacking full-time jobs, many eke out a living as street vendors, selling food, cigarettes, and household items along city streets. Others comb through garbage dumps for food. Most urban children must work to help support their families. Because people are so poor and desperate, crime flourishes in shantytown areas. Pickpockets and other thieves, prostitutes, and drug dealers regularly work the streets of Lima.

Life is quite different for people in mountain areas, where most people are poor. Because of the high mountains, earthquakes, and landslides, it is difficult to build roads and power lines into rural areas. In the Peruvian highlands, the roads are winding, steep, and unpaved. In the wet season, roads turn to mud. When people need to

Some aspects of **urban life in Peru** are similar to those of any other large metropolis. Traffic jams crowd the streets, while pedestrians bustle along the sidewalks.

Most people in **rural Peru** live in brick homes with dirt floors and thatch or tile roofs.

travel, they take rickety buses or ride on trucks used to carry live-stock, crops, and other products.

Few villages have electricity. Many people get water from nearby springs or streams. Some rural towns, particularly those created by the Spanish in colonial times, have a central plaza, a church, cobblestone streets, and a few government offices. Other towns have just a few houses.

Most rural people live in homes made of adobe bricks with floors of packed earth. Roofs are made of adobe tiles or thatch—a mat of grasses and other plant material. Rural people raise llamas, sheep, goats, and cattle, which provide them with meat, milk, and clothing. They grow potatoes and grains for their own use, with little left over to sell. Some people produce handicrafts for sale to tourists. Few people own their own land—most land is owned by the government, big businesses, or other landlords. Rural people have little contact with the cities, although many own portable radios, which provide them with news, sports, and other information.

The Amazon region is different still. It is even more remote than the mountains, yet about 250,000 native people still live there. Traditionally, these people hunted, fished, and gathered wild plants for food. They created pottery, weavings, and other handicrafts. They lived in houses made of branches or poles, with roofs made of thatch. Everything the people needed came from the jungle and its rivers.

In the twentieth century, modern life encroached even into the deepest Amazon. White religious teachers called missionaries tried to convert the natives to Christianity. Logging, mining, pharmaceutical, and oil companies arrived to extract the riches of the jungle. Although some tribes still live as their ancestors did, others have adopted Western-style clothing, weapons, and tools. Some jungle dwellers work on farms and companies operating in the Amazon. Others sell crafts to tourists. Some have moved to the cities.

THE FLOATING ISLANDS

Some of Peru's native peoples still live much like their ancestors did centuries ago. For example, the Uros people, who live on islands in Lake Titicaca, still make fishing boats out of *totora* reeds. In fact, the islands themselves are made of reeds *(below)*. People make these islands, called the Floating Islands, by piling up layers and layers of reeds in the water. As the reeds rot away from the bottom, people replace them on top. The ground is soft and spongy. The biggest of the Floating Islands even holds several buildings—also made of reeds.

CULTURAL LIFE

During the reign of the Incas, Peru had one of the most complex and sophisticated cultures in the world at the time, as evidenced by Inca roadways, architecture, and administrative systems. Inca culture was diminished, and in many ways erased, by the Spaniards, who often built their own churches, government offices, and cities on top of Inca ruins. Slowly, however, Peru has developed a new culture that mixes its Indian past with its Spanish heritage, along with modern cultural influences such as pop music, radio, the Internet, and television.

⊙ Religion

Originally, Indians in Peru practiced traditional religions. They believed in good and evil spirits and worshiped the spirits of nature. Their spiritual leaders were called shamans. The Spanish newcomers, however, belonged to the Roman Catholic Church, and Spanish leaders wanted to spread their faith throughout the Americas. Almost as soon as the first Spaniards arrived in Peru in the sixteenth century,

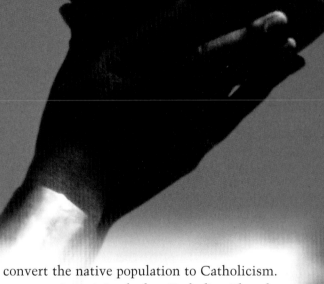

missionaries set out to convert the native population to Catholicism. Over the centuries, many natives joined the Catholic Church, although often against their will. Eventually, Catholicism became the dominant religion in Peru.

In modern times, about 90 percent of the population belongs to the Catholic Church. A minority of Peru's people belong to Protestant churches, such as the Anglican and Methodist Churches, or to other religious groups. The Catholic Church, trying to accommodate the natives, celebrates many masses (religious services) in the native Quechua and Aymara languages.

Despite converting to Catholicism, many Indians also retained some traditional beliefs, such as spirit worship, and these beliefs continue into the twenty-first century. For instance, shamans (curanderos) still operate in many Indian communities, particularly in mountain areas. Many native people still worship mountain gods, called *apus*, as well as Pachamama, or Mother Earth.

A Peruvian priest makes a *hatun hayway*, or "great offering," at Machu Picchu.

Language and Literature

The most commonly spoken language in Peru is Spanish, followed by Quechua, the language of many Indians. Both Spanish and Quechua are official languages of Peru. Quechua is commonly used in rural areas, and some rural schools teach classes in Quechua as well as Spanish. Another native language is Aymara, spoken mainly by Aymara people. Dozens of indigenous tribes in the isolated jungles of eastern Peru speak a variety of other native languages.

Before the Spanish arrived, native people told stories to pass on their histories, legends, and lessons. They did not have any written languages. The Spanish brought their literary traditions to Peru. Several important writers emerged in the Spanish colonial period. Garcilaso de la Vega and Felipe Guamán Poma de Ayala, both mestizos, wrote about life in Peru during the Spanish invasion. Peru's best-known female writer is probably Flora Tristan, a mid-nineteenth-century feminist who fought for the rights of women and workers. Other well-known Peruvian writers include poet César Vallejo. Vallejo, who lived in Paris for much of his life and died in 1938, focused his poetry on Peru's poor and the country's social problems. Among his best-known poems is *The Black Heralds.* Novelist and journalist Ciro Alegría, who studied with Vallejo as a first-grader, also wrote about the troubles of Peru's natives. His best-known work is *Broad and Alien Is the World*, published in 1941.

Mario Vargas Llosa

The most famous modern Peruvian writer is Mario Vargas Llosa, born in Arequipa. Vargas Llosa's fictional works include *Aunt Julia and the Scriptwriter, The War of the End of the World,* and *Conversations in the Cathedral.* Vargas Llosa, who mixes a variety of styles and points of view in his writing, lived in Europe after graduating from college. He returned to Peru and ran for president in 1990. He lost the election to Alberto Fujimori, then moved to Spain.

Music and Dance

Peru's music is diverse because so many different cultural groups have contributed to the tradition. An indigenous Andean musical style called *saya* is very popular in Peru as well as other Latin American countries. The saya sound features flutes, panpipes, and string instruments. *Huayno,* another indigenous form, heard mainly in the mountains, is also very popular. It features a bouncy rhythm. *Criolla* is a combination of African and European rhythms and phrasing. It has been around for centuries, ever since Africans arrived in Peru as slaves, but it became very popular in the twentieth century. It is heard most often along the coast. *Chicha,* best described as Peruvian tropical music, is an urban combination of rock and roll, saya, criolla, huayno, and other Latin forms. Chicha, which began in Peru's taverns, is very popular with the working class. American rock music is also popular in Peru, along with salsa and merengue music from the Caribbean Islands.

Ancient Peruvians made a variety of instruments. Among them are the *zampoña*, or panpipes, a series of hollow reeds cut to different lengths. The *wankara* is a large drum made from a hollow tree trunk and covered by a llama hide. The *charango* is a guitarlike instrument with ten strings and a sound box made from armadillo shell.

Peruvians love to dance. The country's dance culture is centered on traditional, or folk, dancing, often performed at religious or harvest festivals. Peru also has a national ballet company, which combines folkloric dance styles with traditional ballet movements. The dancers usually wear bright, hand-sewn costumes. The *marinera,* considered Peru's national dance, involves a couple twirling around in a mock courtship ritual. The couple holds white handkerchiefs, while musicians provide accompaniment on guitars, drums, and other instruments. Trujillo holds the National Marinera Festival at the end of January.

These children perform **the marinera** during a festival in their town.

Salsa and merengue, with their fast, tropical rhythms, are also popular dance styles. *Salsatecas* (salsa dance halls) are popular in Peru's large cities. Young urban dwellers especially like to dance at parties.

Art and Architecture

Ancient Nazca and Paracas peoples excelled at textile making, especially weaving. Their textiles were woven by hand, using secret techniques. The textiles were sophisticated, with extremely tight weaves, almost two hundred different colors, and patterns showing everyday life in ancient times. Other ancient cultures, especially the Moche, made ceramic figurines, bowls, and pottery. These pieces usually showed people in everyday activities. Modern native Peruvians continue to make tapestries, ceramics, and handicrafts such as dolls. They generally sell these items to tourists at open-air markets or on the street.

In the sixteenth century, native art combined with European styles in a phenomenon called the Cuzco School. Cuzco School artists were indigenous painters who copied great Renaissance works that were being produced in Europe at the time. The Peruvians copied the painting style but with a native flair. Marcos Zapata, for example, redid Leonardo da Vinci's painting *The Last Supper.* Zapata's work showed Jesus and the apostles, just like the original painting, but he also inserted Peruvian foods, including guinea pig, onto the dinner table.

Photography arrived in Peru in the late nineteenth century. The country's most famous photographer is Martín Chambi. He was born in 1891 in a small village in southern Peru. As a young man, he met a photographer at a gold mine, who taught him the basics of his art. From 1920 to 1950, Chambi photographed the rich, the poor, and the natural wonders of his country. He was among the first to photograph Indians in everyday life. He was also the first to photograph the ruins of Machu Picchu.

Peru's history is evident in its architecture. In many cities, especially the larger ones, modern hotels or office buildings stand next to colonial-era churches and even Inca walls. The Incas were master builders. Their buildings, especially religious and military structures, were often built in the shape of animals such as jaguars. Inca builders cut building stones into giant squares, often weighing a ton or more each. The stones fit together so tightly that the builders didn't need to use mortar to hold them in place. The fit remains so tight that even in modern times, you can't insert a knife into the joint between two stones. Inca buildings are able to withstand the country's many earthquakes, while many Spanish and more modern structures are not.

Inca structures are remarkably strong because of the snug fit of their stones. Despite hundreds of years and many devastating earthquakes, Inca-era buildings still stand.

In many Peruvian towns, colonial and modern builders constructed new buildings atop foundations built by Inca engineers, especially in Cuzco. The Spanish brought their own style of architecture to Peru. This style included tiled roofs, large interior patios, and thick adobe walls. Ornate colonial buildings are seen throughout Lima and other large cities.

> For links where you can find out more about Peruvian traditions, cultural life, literature, music, dance, current events, cuisine, and much more, go to vgsbooks.com.

Modern Media

Dozens of newspapers are published in Peru on a daily or weekly basis. *El Comericio,* published in Lima, offers good coverage of national and international news, as do *Expreso* and *La República.* Peru has thirteen television stations, which offer a variety of dramas, comedies, sports, and news shows. *Telenovelas,* or soap operas, many of them produced in Mexico or Brazil, are particularly popular. Radio stations broadcast in both Spanish and Quechua. Even in the most remote parts of the mountains, many families have portable radios. Although telephone and Internet service are available in Peru, few Peruvians can afford phones or computers. Only a small percentage of Peruvians have access to home or cellular phones.

Peru's newsstands offer dozens of newspapers and magazines.

With their faces painted the color of Peru's flag, **Peruvian soccer fans** cheer for their team during a qualifying match for the World Cup.

▶ Sports and Recreation

Soccer is king in Peru, as it is in many Latin American countries. The country has numerous teams playing at all levels—from pickup matches to professional competition. It is not unusual to see children playing the game almost anywhere, from Pacific beaches to Andean villages. The most popular and best teams are in Lima. The national team plays all over the world and occasionally qualifies for the World Cup tournament.

Another popular sport, especially among women, is volleyball. Peru's women's national team has had great success in international competitions. In 1988 the women won a silver medal at the Summer Olympic Games in Seoul, South Korea. Other popular sports include fishing and surfing along the Pacific coast, which has large waves.

Early Peruvian textiles and pottery show images of people surfing. These items are about two thousand years old—the oldest images of surfing ever found—so Peru claims to be the birthplace of surfing.

Each year around Easter, the village of Huanchaco hosts the National Surfing Championship, which has become internationally famous. Other forms of entertainment, such as bullfighting and cockfighting, come from the Spanish tradition.

Peruvians also enjoy social interactions, such as family gatherings and visiting with neighbors. A favorite pastime in small towns is an evening stroll around the town square. Peruvians enjoy watching movies, either in the theater or on video. Few films have been made in Peru, however.

Food and Drink

Peru has a varied cuisine, with potatoes and corn forming the staples of the diet. Native people have grown these foods for thousands of years. Potatoes are especially popular, and hundreds of different varieties grow around the country. Fish and llama meat have been part of the Peruvian diet since ancient times. The Spanish invaders brought cows, pigs, and goats to Peru. As a result, beef, pork, and goat meat became part of the Peruvian diet as well. Peruvians also eat fruits such as tomatoes. They eat a lot of grains, especially a native grain called quinoa. Quinoa can be cooked and eaten like rice, or ground into flour. It has twice the protein of other grains.

Different regions of the country specialize in different types of foods. The coast, of course, contributes seafood, while the mountains offer dishes made with llama meat. The jungles provide a wide variety of fruits, such as mangoes. *Cuy,* or guinea pig, is traditionally prepared for festivals and other special occasions. *Charqui,* made from llama meat that has been dried and cured like beef jerky, is popular in the mountains. Another popular traditional dish is *pachamanca,* prepared

Fruits and vegetables form a large part of the Peruvian diet. Many Peruvians buy their fresh produce in open-air markets such as this one in Puno.

in an underground oven. To make this dish, villagers dig a hole in the ground and place wood inside to make a fire. They put large, clean stones on top of the fire. Meat and vegetables are then placed on top of the hot stones to cook.

Peruvian cooking features a lot of spices, which make the food hot and zesty. One of the most popular condiments is *ají,* made of hot peppers and lemon juice or vegetable oil. Among the favorite drinks in Peru is *chicha,* an alcoholic drink made from fermented corn. The most popular bottled soft drink is Inca Kola, a sweet soda made from various fruits.

PAPAS À LA HUANCAINA

Potatoes originated in South America, so it is not surprising that they are used a lot in Peruvian cooking. Dozens of different types of potatoes grow in the country. *Papa* is the Spanish word for "potato," and one of the most popular dishes in Peru is *papas à la huancaina.* The dish is considered a main course. It takes about an hour to prepare.

10 medium potatoes (new or red)

1 lb. cheese (Romano, Mexican, or feta)

2 small jalapeño peppers

1 c. evaporated milk

½ c. vegetable oil

2 cloves whole garlic, peeled

8 saltine crackers

1 tbsp. Dijon mustard

salt and pepper to taste

head of lettuce

3 hard-boiled eggs, peeled

black olives

1. Bring a large pan of water to a boil.
2. Meanwhile, peel the potatoes and cut them in half.
3. Add the potatoes to the water with a pinch of salt. Cook on high heat for 15 to 20 minutes, or until tender. Drain the potatoes and let them cool.
4. In a blender, mix the cheese, peppers, evaporated milk, oil, garlic, crackers, and mustard to make a thick sauce. Add salt and pepper to taste.
5. Lay a bed of lettuce leaves in a serving dish and place the potatoes on top. Cover them with the sauce.
6. Cut the hard-boiled eggs in half and place on top of the potatoes and sauce. Add black olives if desired. Serve slightly cold. Serves 6 or more.

DRESSED FOR THE OCCASION

In big cities such as Lima, people dress a lot like North Americans, with casual slacks, dresses, and other Western-style clothing. In the Andes, however, many people still wear the traditional dress of their ancestors. For women, this clothing includes bright, multilayered petticoats called *polleras*; colorful, alpaca wool sweaters; and delicately woven belts. Men wear heavy ponchos spun from cotton or vicuña wool, often with elaborate geometric designs. Many people wear round woolen hats with curved brims. In cold parts of the Andes, people wear *chullos*, woolen caps with earflaps and colorful decorations. For dances and other special occasions, people wear more elaborate costumes.

○ Holidays and Festivals

Peru has thirteen public holidays and many unofficial celebrations. Almost everyone observes the major Catholic holidays. Holy Thursday, Good Friday, and Easter Sunday are all part of Semana Santa, or Holy Week. Holy Week celebrations include reenactments of the crucifixion of Jesus, as well as candlelight processions each night. The best known Semana Santa festival is held in Ayacucho.

On June 29, people in Peru honor Saint Peter and Saint Paul—leaders of the early Christian Church. On August 30, Peruvians honor Saint Rose of Lima, the first saint in the Americas. December 25 is Christmas.

Other major holidays are New Year's Day (January 1), Labor Day (May 1), and the Day of the Peasant (June 24). July 28 and 29 are reserved to celebrate Peru's independence from Spain. October 8 celebrates the 1879 Battle of Angamos, during which Peru defeated Spain at sea. November 1 is All Saints' Day, which honors the country's dead.

These children are dressed in **traditional clothing.** The girl is wearing a pollera, and the boy is wearing a poncho and chullo.

A man portraying **the Inca king leads the Inti Raymi festival** every year at the ruins of Sacsayhuamán. Dressed in their finest Quechua clothing, participants welcome the Inca new year with festivities lasting one week.

Just about every village, town, and city has a patron saint—the saint who is said to protect that place. People honor their patron saint with a festival that can last several days. During the festival, people often carry a statue of the saint through the city. The parade is led by the majordomo, a church member elected to plan and raise money for the festival. Patron saint celebrations often feature a *castillo*, or fireworks castle. The castillo is a wooden tower layered with fireworks and placed in the town square. Crowds gather to watch the colorful fireworks display.

Along with church and patriotic festivities, Peruvians also celebrate their indigenous past. Most notable and important is the Inti Raymi festival. Inti Raymi, also called the Festival of the Sun, takes place in June each year. It marks the Inca new year. People all over the country dress in traditional Quechua costumes—including white shirts, knit caps, and billowing skirts (for women). Inca-style dances take place in towns and villages. The biggest ceremony is held at the ancient Inca site of Sacsayhuamán near Cuzco. A man selected to play the part of the Inca king leads the celebration. Inti Raymi celebrations last for a week.

THE ECONOMY

Throughout its history, Peru has been blessed with valuable natural resources—including precious metals and a great fishing industry. But the country has not been able to take advantage of those resources to improve the lives of the majority of its people. Even during the time of the Incas, wealth was not evenly distributed. Under the mita system, common people were provided with food and shelter in exchange for work. But the king owned and controlled all the empire's wealth.

The lives of the native people worsened when the Spaniards took over. Not only was the Inca Empire crushed, but its wealth was shipped to Spain for the benefit of the Spanish king. The Incas became near-slaves, with no guarantee of food or shelter.

Even after independence in the nineteenth century, the economic situation did not improve much. While Peruvians were free of Spanish control, political problems, wars, and government corruption kept the country in financial trouble much of the time. The result was slow economic development and too much foreign

intervention in Peruvian affairs. Peru went deeply into debt with international bankers and businesspeople.

During the twentieth century, economic troubles continued. The military held political power for much of the century. By the time civilian control was restored in the 1980s, Peru was faced with growing debt and attacks from rebel groups. These pressures caused the economy to crumble. International financial organizations such as the World Bank and the International Monetary Fund stopped making loans to Peru because it was so far behind on its debt payments. Inflation skyrocketed in 1990. Foreigners were hesitant to invest in the country because of the violence of the Shining Path and other rebel groups.

It was not until the election of President Alberto Fujimori that the economy and the violence were brought under control. Fujimori arrested rebel leaders, diminishing the influence of the Shining Path. He strengthened the nation's banking system, increased international trade, and began selling government-owned enterprises to private buyers.

A World Without Money

It is said that money makes the world go 'round, but that was not true of the Incas and their empire. Money did not exist in the Inca Empire because the people had no need for it. The king owned everything, and the government provided everything people needed, including food and housing, in exchange for their work. Coins made of precious metals were introduced in Peru by Spaniards in the sixteenth century. The Spaniards first made silver coins in Lima in 1598. They started making gold coins in 1675. Modern Peruvians use a unit of currency called the nuevo sol, issued as both coins and paper notes.

Inflation dropped to reasonable levels in the 1990s, and the economy grew. By 1997 the country's yearly gross domestic product (GDP), the total value of its goods and services, had grown to $54 billion. Per capita income (the amount the average person earns in a year) was $2,150.

But as the twentieth century came to an end, more problems developed. An El Niño weather current hit in 1998, causing massive flooding and slowing the economy once more. About the same time, a financial crisis hit Asia, where Peru does a lot of business. Asia's financial problems further slowed Peru's economy. By 2002 per capita income had increased to $2,390, but most people remained at or below the poverty line. As people struggled to make a living, they tried to make money outside the legal economy. Some people sold goods and services on the street. Others participated in the illegal buying and selling of drugs such as cocaine.

◎ Agriculture

Peru's agriculture is far from modernized. Most Peruvians farm much as their ancestors did, with few mechanized tools and using animals such as llamas to carry heavy loads. In addition, the country's rough terrain limits the amount of agriculture that takes place—only about 2.8 percent of the land is suitable for farming. Still, agriculture (including farming, fishing, and forestry) has always been the largest employer in the country. About 33 percent of Peru's workforce makes a living by farming or fishing. Agriculture accounts for about 10 percent of the nation's GDP.

Peru's main agricultural crops are sugarcane, potatoes, rice, plantains, corn, and cotton. Coffee is also an important crop, accounting for about 6 percent of the nation's export earnings. Farmers also grow wheat, vegetables, and fruit. Most crops are grown in the fertile valleys of the coast and the mountains. Coffee is grown high in the Andes. Many farmers also raise livestock, including poultry, sheep, cattle, pigs, and goats.

Farming remains Peru's chief employer. These farmers are plowing their field, located in the Urubamba River valley.

People in the Andes Mountains raise llamas and alpacas, which provide meat for food and wool for textiles and also serve as beasts of burden. The jungle regions also are sources of rubber, medicines, and valuable hardwood. Many farmers operate illegal coca farms in cleared areas of the jungle—the coca is then processed to make cocaine. Some areas of the jungle have also been cleared for coffee farming.

Given Peru's long coastline on the Pacific Ocean, it is not surprising that Peru is one of the five largest producers of fish in the world, with more than 4 million tons (3.6 million metric tons) caught each year. Anchovies and pilchards (fish resembling a herring) are the most harvested fish. Peru also produces a large amount of fish meal—dried, ground-up fish used for fertilizer and feeding livestock. Much of this fish meal is sold to other countries, accounting for about 12.5 percent of the total value of Peru's exports.

Industry

Peru's industry, which includes mining, manufacturing, construction, and power generation, contributes about 27 percent of Peru's gross domestic product. Industry employs nearly 2 million people. A large portion of the country's industry, about 70 percent, is located in the metropolitan area of Lima.

Minerals, especially copper and silver, have traditionally been one of Peru's greatest resources. In fact, Peru is among the world's biggest

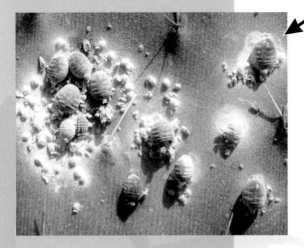

Cochineal insects feed on only the prickly pear cactus. The insects emit a white, waxy substance over their feeding area to camouflage themselves from predators. The red fluid used for dye is stored inside the insect's body fluids and tissues.

RED DYE NUMBER ONE

One of Peru's best money-makers is carmine, a red dye that is used all over the world. Carmine comes from the female cochineal, a small desert insect that lives on the prickly pear cactus. The dye is made from crushed, dried cochineals. Peru is the world's largest cochineal exporter. The dye is used to color clothing, paint, makeup, lipstick, food, and hot dogs.

producers of copper, silver, lead, and zinc. Peru also has deposits of gold, iron ore, coal, and phosphates. Mining accounts for about 10 percent of Peru's GDP, and about 2.5 percent of Peruvians are employed in mining. Peru has oil wells, mainly in the jungle and on its northern coast. A large refinery, or factory for processing oil, is located near the city of Talara in the north, in the heart of the coastal oil fields. Natural gas production is heavy along the central coast.

The manufacturing sector includes food processing and the production of chemicals, textiles, cement, automobiles, ships, plastics, legal drugs, and electronic goods. Manufacturing contributes about 15 percent of the nation's GDP while employing more than 800,000 people. This sector was hard hit by the economic problems of the 1990s. The downturn lasted through 2001, but government figures show that the situation is improving. In fact, manufacturing and construction are among the best performing sectors of the economy.

◉ Services

The services sector, such as office work, tourism, communications, and sales, makes up more than 60 percent of the nation's gross domestic product, employing more than 4 million people. The tourism industry is growing, as millions of people come to Peru each year to visit Inca ruins or to wander the nation's beaches, mountains, and jungles. These travelers are part of a growing trend called ecotourism, which involves visiting natural places, creating limited disturbance of the land or wildlife there. Peru's tourism revenues are approaching $1 billion per year. The biggest problem for tourism is Peru's lack of roads, which makes getting around the country difficult. Although terrorists operate in some remote areas, tourists are generally safe in Peru.

Iquitos is the largest city in the jungles of Peru. It is the starting point for most tourists visiting the Amazon River. In the nineteenth century, Iquitos was the center of the rubber boom. Starting in 1880, the demand for rubber increased so much that landowners with rubber trees became rich. The rubber barons, as they were called, built great houses. The rubber boom ended in 1912.

Foreign Trade

Peru's main imports are food, machinery, metals, chemicals, petroleum, and motor vehicles. Most imports, which value more than $7 billion per year, come from the United States, Japan, Colombia, Venezuela, Brazil, Argentina, South Korea, Germany, and China. The United States is by far the biggest source of imports, providing goods to Peru worth more than $2.2 billion annually, more than four times greater than Japan at number two.

Peru's main exports are coffee, fish meal, cotton, sugar, and minerals. The main markets for exports, which total more than $5.6 billion annually, are the United States, Switzerland, the United Kingdom, Germany, and China. Again, the United States is by far

Workers sort through cotton in a cotton factory. The cotton is being processed for the Land's End clothing company in the United States. The United States is Peru's largest export partner.

the largest export partner, buying more than $1.8 billion in Peruvian exports each year.

◉ Illegal Economic Activities

The most lucrative illegal activity in Peru is the harvesting of coca plants, which are processed into a paste and then into the illegal drug cocaine. Processing takes place both in Peru and in other countries. During the late 1980s and early 1990s, Peru made more money from illegally exporting coca paste than through its legal exports. Law enforcement officials estimate that at one time, as many as 320,000 coca growers operated in the country, as well as 107,000 paste processors and almost 500,000 workers in the production and refining of cocaine. These people supported more than 2.5 million family members, or about 10 percent of the country's total population. Although this moneymaking activity helped some Peruvians, it also led to crime, violence, and drug addiction. The Peruvian government cracked down on illegal coca growers, and by the end of the twentieth century, cocaine production had been cut in half.

Many Peruvians sell goods and services illegally as part of an underground, or black market, economy. Social researchers, including author Mario Vargas Llosa, estimate that hundreds of thousands of people engage in this activity in Lima alone. Some of them are

A police officer throws a **bag containing cocaine** into a fire. Many tons of illegal drugs are burned in Peru each year.

skilled professionals, such as plumbers and electricians, who make money outside of government control, avoiding taxes and regulations. Others are simply street vendors who peddle food and other goods without licenses. The results for customers are usually cheaper prices for goods and services, but also no legal protections if a job is done badly or if a product breaks.

 At vgsbooks.com, you'll find the latest information on the Peruvian economy, in addition to a converter where you can see the current exchange rate and convert U.S. dollars into nuevo sol.

The Future

The late 1990s and the early 2000s were difficult years for Peru. El Niño hit in 1998, causing widespread flooding and limiting economic growth. A financial crisis that hit Asia also took its toll on Peru, and the turmoil surrounding the reelection of President Alberto Fujimori created much uncertainty. This turmoil only worsened when Fujimori was found unfit for office after a political scandal.

But life is not completely bleak in Peru. The future looks better than the past for a variety of reasons. The economy is less restricted, as the government has sold off industries that it once owned, including telecommunications, electrical, and mining businesses. This change should improve the efficiency of those industries, as private owners seek to reduce costs and increase profits. It should also create more jobs, as well as improved service for Peruvians, as the industries try to grow and attract more customers. The World Bank has again extended credit to Peru, and the economy is starting to rebound. The country's GDP has grown to $60.3 billion, and per capita income is up slightly.

Finally, the political situation has stabilized with the election of Alejandro Toledo. In 2002 he obtained a $50 million loan from the World Bank to build better water systems and sanitation services for Peru. The former World Bank economist and the first Indian to be elected president, Toledo promises to help develop good economic policies that will lead Peru to a brighter future.

Timeline

CA. 8000 B.C. Peru's earliest inhabitants arrive.

CA. 2500 B.C. Peruvians build villages along the Pacific coast.

CA. 1800 B.C. Peruvians move inland, creating villages in the mountains.

CA. 800 B.C. Chavín culture dominates the region.

CA. 100 B.C. The Nazca begin creating their designs in the desert.

CA. A.D. 100 The Moche rule along the northern coast.

CA. 300 The Lord of Sipán is buried along with great riches.

CA. 1200 The Incas begin to expand their empire in southern Peru.

CA. 1300 The city of Chan Chan is built.

1400s The Inca Empire reaches its peak.

1530 Atahualpa takes control of the Inca Empire. Francisco Pizarro returns to Peru.

1533 Led by Pizarro, a Spanish force kills Atahualpa. Peru becomes a possession of Spain.

1535 Pizarro creates a new Peruvian capital, which comes to be called Lima.

1541 Pizarro is killed in Lima by fellow Spaniards.

1551 The National Autonomous University of San Marcos is founded in Lima. It is the first university in the Americas.

1572 Spanish authorities arrest and kill Túpac Amaru, the last Inca ruler.

1671 The Pope canonizes Rose of Lima, the first saint born in the Americas.

1746 An earthquake demolishes most of Lima, killing four thousand people.

1820 José de San Martín enters Peru with his army to fight for Peruvian independence.

1821 Peru declares independence from Spain.

1824 Simón Bolívar becomes president of Peru.

1827 Peru's first constitution goes into effect.

1840 The guano boom begins.

1849 Chinese and Japanese workers arrive to work on Peru's farms and railroads.

1879 War breaks out between Peru, Chile, and Bolivia. Peru loses land in the fighting.

1880   The rubber boom begins.

1919   Augusto Leguía assumes control of Peru as dictator.

1924   The American Popular Revolutionary Alliance (APRA) is founded.

1932   A labor protest in Trujillo leaves hundreds of APRA members dead.

1950   An earthquake hits Cuzco, killing an estimated thirty-five thousand people.

1963   Fernando Belaúnde Terry is elected president, ending military rule.

1968   Quechua is recognized as the second official language of Peru. General Juan Velasco Alvarado takes over the government.

1970   A severe earthquake in northern Peru kills about fifty thousand people.

1980   The Shining Path begins a terrorist campaign against the government.

1983   The El Niño weather pattern causes widespread flooding and other damage.

1985   Alan García Pérez is elected president. He pushes for police and military reforms.

1988   Peru's women's volleyball team wins a silver medal at the 1988 Olympics in Seoul, South Korea.

1990   Alberto Fujimori is elected president.

1992   Fujimori suspends the constitution and assumes greater power.

1993   Peru adopts a new constitution, allowing Fujimori to seek reelection.

1998   El Niño again devastates coastal Peru.

2000   Fujimori resigns after a bribery scandal in his administration and flees to Japan.

2001   Alejandro Toledo is elected president. The Peruvian government brings accusations of murder and kidnapping against Fujimori.

2003   Explorers discover lost Inca city of Llactapata near Machu Picchu. Peru's government asks Japan to hand over Fujimori so he can be tried in Lima for his alleged crimes.

COUNTRY NAME Republic of Peru

AREA 496,225 square miles (1,285,222 sq. km)

MAIN LANDFORMS Pacific coast, Andes Mountains, the selva (jungle)

HIGHEST POINT Mount Huascarán, 22,205 feet (6,768 m) above sea level

LOWEST POINT Sea level

MAJOR RIVERS Amazon, Ucayali, Marañón, Napo, Tigre, Pastaza, Pachitea, Urubamba, Madre de Dios, Tambopata, Huallaga

ANIMALS Llamas, alpacas, vicuñas, parrots, jaguars, monkeys, toucans, condors, river otters, anteaters, spectacled bears

CAPITAL CITY Lima

OTHER MAJOR CITIES Cuzco, Arequipa, Trujillo, Iquitos

OFFICIAL LANGUAGES Spanish, Quechua

MONETARY UNIT Nuevo sol. 1 nuevo sol = 100 centimos

PERUVIAN CURRENCY

The nuevo sol is the official currency of Peru. Bills come in denominations of 10, 20, 50, 100, and 200 nuevo sols. The bills each show a famous person on the front and a scene from Peruvian culture on the back. Coins come in denominations of 1, 2, and 5 nuevo sols. Other coins come in 5, 10, 20, and 50 centimos. In big cities, people will accept U.S. dollars as readily as nuevo sols.

The Peruvian flag consists of three vertical (upright) bars—a white one in the center surrounded by red ones. The red stands for the blood of Peruvians who fought and died to gain the country's independence from Spain in the nineteenth century. The white bar includes a coat of arms made up of a shield surrounded by a green wreath. The shield features pictures of a vicuña; a cinchona tree, the source of quinine; and a cornucopia, or horn of plenty, overflowing with gold coins. These items symbolize Peru's flora, fauna, and mineral riches. The flag of Peru was adopted in 1825.

"Marcha Nacional," the national anthem of Peru, dates to the country's independence in 1821, but it was not officially adopted until 1913. The song speaks of the long history of oppression the Peruvian people suffered and how they were still able to lift their heads with pride. The lyrics were written in Spanish by José Bernardo Alzedo, with some rewriting by Claudio Rebagliati in 1869. The music was written by José de la Torre Ugarte. Here is an English translation of the first verse and chorus.

> We are free; let us always be so, let us always be so.
> Let the sun rather deny its light,
> Than that we should fail the solemn vow,
> Which our country raised to God.
>
> For a long time the Peruvian, oppressed,
> Dragged the ominous chain;
> Condemned to cruel serfdom,
> For a long time, for a long time, for a long time he moaned in silence.
> But as soon as the sacred cry of
> Freedom! was heard on his coasts,
> He shook off the indolence of the slave,
> He raised his humiliated, his humiliated, his humiliated head.
> He raised, he raised his humiliated head.

For a link where you can listen to Peru's national anthem, go to vgsbooks.com.

SUSANA BACA (b. 1954) Among Peru's most famous modern singers is Susana Baca, an Afro-Peruvian musician. Baca was born in Chorrillos. Both her parents were also musicians. She released her first solo album, *Susana Baca*, in 1998. Her work consists of folk tunes, new songs, and poems set to music. She is popular in Peru as well as North America and Europe.

SERGIO BAMBARÉN (b. 1960) Born in Lima, Bambarén has found fame as a writer of magical stories for adults and children. After growing up in Peru, Bambarén attended college in the United States. He then moved to Portugal, Australia, and finally back to Lima. *Dolphin— Story of a Dreamer* is his best-known work. The beautifully illustrated book, which tells of a dolphin's search for the "perfect wave," has sold one million copies worldwide.

FERNANDO BELAÚNDE TERRY (1912–2002) A successful architect, Belaúnde Terry was twice president of Peru and was considered a champion of democracy. He was born in Arequipa and earned a degree in architecture from the University of Texas. He formed the Popular Action Party in 1956. Elected president of Peru in 1963, he instituted educational and land reforms. Bad economic times led to the military takeover of his government in 1968. He then moved to the United States and taught architecture at Harvard and Columbia universities. He returned to Peru and was elected president again in 1980, ending years of military rule.

MARTÍN CHAMBI (1891–1973) Born in a small village in the Andes, Chambi was one of the greatest photographers in history and the first famous indigenous photographer in Latin America. He specialized in picturing natives in their daily lives, as well as the culture and architecture of Peru. He was the first to photograph Machu Picchu. His photos have been shown all over the world.

ALAN GARCÍA PÉREZ (b. 1949) Born in Lima, García became president of Peru in 1985, the youngest man ever to win the office. He had studied in Lima, as well as in Spain and France. He was elected to Peru's congress in 1978. A moderate leftist, he created social and economic reforms but lost control of the economy, resulting in runaway inflation. He was replaced by Alberto Fujimori.

JAVIER PÉREZ DE CUELLAR (b. 1920) One of the most famous politicians in Peru's history, Pérez represented Peru at the first United Nations meeting in 1946. Born in Lima, he was the first Latin American to be named secretary-general of the United Nations, taking the job in 1982. Prior to joining the UN, Pérez studied at the University of Lima and worked as a lawyer. At the UN, he helped end the Iran-Iraq

War (1980–1988). He ran for president of Peru in 1995 but was defeated by Alberto Fujimori.

YMA SUMAC (b. 1921?) Mystery has surrounded this singer right from her birth, which took place sometime between 1921 and 1928. Sumac was born Zoila Emperatriz Chavarri del Castillo in Inchocan. She claims to be descended from Inca royalty. She began performing on radio in Peru in her early teens. In 1947 Sumac moved to New York City and signed with Capitol Records in 1950, reaching her biggest fame in the 1950s and 1960s. Also an actress, Sumac has appeared on Broadway and in Hollywood movies. Among her films are *Secret of the Incas* and *Omar Khayyam.*

ALEJANDRO TOLEDO MANRIQUE (b. 1946) In 2001 Toledo became the first Indian to become president of Peru. He was born to poor parents in Cabana in rural Peru and grew up in the city of Chimbote. He was talented enough to win scholarships to the University of San Francisco, Harvard, and Stanford—all in the United States. He taught business and worked as an official with the World Bank before being elected president.

FLORA TRISTAN (1803–1844) Born in Paris to a Peruvian father and a French mother, Tristan traveled extensively in Peru. She wrote novels and memoirs documenting the plight of women in European and Latin American society. Her most famous work is *Peregrinations of a Pariah,* which examines the lives of downtrodden women in Lima.

TÚPAC AMARU (1742–1781) Born José Gabriel Condorcanqui in Cuzco, he assumed the name of the last Inca king and led the indigenous people of Peru in revolt against Spain. An educated man, he also wanted to change conditions for Indians in the mills, mines, and fields. His rebellion started in 1780, but the Spaniards soon captured and executed him and his family. His capture marked the end of Inca uprisings in Peru.

MARIO VARGAS LLOSA (b. 1936) Born in Arequipa, Vargas Llosa is the best known Peruvian novelist and one of the most innovative writers in the world. Like many Latin writers, his works feature magical elements that twist reality. Among his works are *The Time of the Hero, Aunt Julia and the Scriptwriter, The War of the End of the World,* and *The Feast of the Goat.* Hoping to take advantage of his fame, Vargas Llosa ran for president of Peru in 1990. In a major upset, he lost to the then little known Alberto Fujimori.

CHAN CHAN The largest adobe, or mud brick, city in the world, Chan Chan is located near Trujillo. It was built by the Chimú people around A.D. 1300. Visitors to the site will see ancient adobe walls, burial mounds, and other structures.

CHAVÍN DE HUÁNTAR This 2,500-year-old fortress temple is considered to be one of Peru's most important pre-Columbian sites. The site features the ruins of stone temples, staircases, and sculptures. It also holds extensive underground chambers and passageways.

CONVENT OF SAN FRANCISCO Located in Lima, the convent was built in the seventeenth century. It was used as a burial site before cemeteries were built around Lima. It has twenty-five thousand skeletons in its underground tombs, as well as twenty-five thousand rare books in its library. The convent was damaged in a 1970 earthquake, but it has since been restored to its original ornate appearance.

FLOATING ISLANDS Situated in Lake Titicaca, the floating islands are made of totora reeds, as are the buildings on the island. The people who live there also make their boats from totora reeds, just as their ancestors did centuries ago. The local people sell souvenirs to tourists and sometimes even give rides in their reed boats.

LAKE TITICACA The highest navigable lake in the world, Titicaca is 12,500 feet (3,810 m) above sea level. In the Andes Mountains, the lake forms part of the border between Peru and Bolivia. Most visitors to the area like to take a boat trip on the lake. They might see alpacas and llamas nearby, as well as colorful birds such as flamingos.

MACHU PICCHU This legendary lost city of the Incas was rediscovered in 1911 by explorer Hiram Bingham. Famous for its extensive ruins, it was probably a center of worship or a home for Inca rulers. The site includes ancient stone tombs, temples, staircases, and plazas. A highlight is the Temple of the Sun, a stunning example of Inca stone work. On Winter Solstice (June 21), the sun shines perfectly through one of the temple's windows. Archaeologists have not yet determined how the Inca knew the precise location of the sun during solstice.

NAZCA LINES Made by the Nazca Indians, the lines are patterns, spirals, and animal figures that go on for miles on the desert floor. More than two thousand years old, the drawings were rediscovered in the 1920s. Most people who come to see the lines take an airplane flight for the best view. But you can also see some of the designs from an observation tower north of Nazca.

SACSAYHUAMÁN This giant Inca fortress is made of stone blocks, one of which weighs more than 300 tons (272 metric tons). The site is also home to the annual Inti Raymi festival, held every June 24.

black market: illegal trade in goods and services, operating without government regulation

colony: a region ruled by a foreign power, often with settlers from the foreign nation overseeing day-to-day governance and business

Communism: a political system in which the government controls all economic activity, with no private property or free enterprise

deforestation: the process of clearing forests to harvest timber or to create farmland

ecotourism: visiting natural places, creating limited disturbance of the land and wildlife there

encomienda: during Spanish colonization of Peru, a system under which the Spanish king entrusted tracts of land (and Indians to work the land) to loyal Spanish settlers

epiphyte: a plant that gets moisture and the materials needed to make its food from the air and rain. Epiphytes usually grow on another plant.

gross domestic product (GDP): a measure of the total value of goods and services produced within a country in a certain amount of time (usually one year). A similar measurement is gross national product (GNP). GDP and GNP are often measured in terms of purchasing power parity (PPP). PPP converts values to international dollars, making it possible to compare how much similar goods and services cost to the residents of different countries.

indigenous: native to a specific country. The Indians of Peru, for instance, are considered indigenous peoples.

irrigation: a system of pipes, canals, and pumps used to carry water to crops

leftist: leaning toward liberal political views. Leftists often favor the rights of poor people over big business and the rich.

missionaries: religious teachers who try to convert others to their faith

nationalize: to seize private industry and turn it over to government control

pre-Columbian: occurring before Christopher Columbus and other Europeans arrived in the Americas

privatize: to sell government-controlled industry to private businesses

tribute: payment made to a landlord or other authority, often exacted by force

Selected Bibliography

Box, Ben, and Alan Murphy. *Peru Handbook.* **Bath, U.K.: Footprint Handbooks Ltd., 2001.**
This thorough travel book offers lots of interesting details about Peru's history, society, and environment.

Central Intelligence Agency (CIA), "Peru," *The World Fact Book.*
Website: <http://www.cia.gov/cia/publications/factbook/geos/pe.html> **(April 2003)**
Although no deep analysis is provided, this site has a wealth of information on the basic political, social, and economic infrastructures of Peru.

Clayton, Lawrence A. *Peru and the United States: The Condor and the Eagle.* **Athens: University of Georgia Press, 1999.**
Clayton, who grew up in Peru, takes a comprehensive look at the long history between the two countries. The book looks at issues such as the illegal cocaine trade, the Shining Path guerrilla movement, and President Alberto Fujimori's impact on the country.

Cultures of the Andes
Website: <http://www.andes.org> **(November 2003)**
This is one of the most varied websites about Peru and life in the Andes. It features not only a variety of photographs of everyday life, but also a collection of songs, songs, jokes, riddles, poetry, and basic lessons in the Quechua language. It also has short stories, a list of resources, and a lot of links to other Andean sites. The information is presented in English, Spanish, and Quechua.

The Europa World Year Book. **London: Europa Publications Limited, 2001.**
This book offers annual statistics about countries of the world. It includes data on population, trade, transportation, political parties, and the media in Peru. It also contains a long article on recent developments in Peru.

Hemming, John. *The Conquest of the Incas.* **New York: Harcourt Brace Jovanovich, 1970.**
This book offers a good description of how the Spaniards conquered the Incas and the hostility that developed between the conquerors and the natives in Peru.

Klaren, Peter F. *Peru: Society and Nationhood in the Andes.* **New York: Oxford University Press, 2000.**
This book looks at the rise and fall of the Incas, the Spanish occupation, and the problems of independence in Peru. It focuses on the social, economic, and political conditions that have shaped modern Peru. The book includes a good bibliography.

Parker, D. S. *The Idea of the Middle Class: White-Collar Workers and Peruvian Society, 1900–1950.* **University Park, PA: Pennsylvania State University Press, 1998.**
This book takes a thorough look at the lifestyle, values, and attitudes of Peru's middle class.

Population Reference Bureau, 2003.
Website: <http://www.prb.org> **(April 2003)**
This site contains a searchable database filled with demographic information for all countries on earth, including Peru.

Prescott, William H. *History of the Conquest of Mexico and History of the Conquest of Peru.* **New York: Cooper Square Press, 2000.**
This massive work is considered a classic by some but a bit dated by others. The author cites a lot of original sources. His words read like a historical novel.

The Statesman's Yearbook. **New York: St. Martin's Press, 2001.**
Published each year since 1863, this reference work contains updated information on major political, business, and economic changes in the world's countries, including Peru. It includes biographical information on world leaders.

Vargas Llosa, Mario. *A Fish in the Water.* **New York: Farrar Strauss and Giroux, 1994.**
This is the memoir of Peru's best known author. The book focuses on Vargas Llosa's unsuccessful run for president against little known Alberto Fujimori in 1990. It also touches on how Vargas Llosa became a writer.

Bingham, Hiram. *Lost City of the Incas: The Story of Machu Picchu and Its Builders.* **New York: Duell, Sloan and Pearce, 1948.**
This firsthand account tells of the famous archaeologist's discovery of Machu Picchu in 1911. It reads like an adventure story.

Congress of the Republic of Peru
Website: <http://www.cobgreso.gob.pe/en/index.asp>
This government site includes information about current events in Peru, the constitution, history, and more.

Corona, Laurel. *Peru.* **San Diego: Lucent Books, 2001.**
This title offers a comprehensive look at Peru and its society. The book focuses on Peru's economy, politics, and daily life.

Eagen, James. *The Aymara of South America.* **Minneapolis: Lerner Publications Company, 2002.**
This book examines the culture and lifestyle of the Aymara people, one of Peru's indigenous groups. Illustrated with abundant color photos, the book explores how the Aymara have maintained their traditions in the fast-paced, modern world.

Heisey, Janet. *Peru.* **Milwaukee: Gareth Stevens Publishing, 2001.**
This book for young readers offers a brief overview of Peru, its institutions, and its cultures. It also looks at Peru's relations with North America.

The Inca Empire
Website: <http://www.theincas.com/history/empire_map.htm>
At this website, you can learn about Inca history, culture, religion, and more. View maps showing where they lived and see artifacts of the Inca that have been discovered by scientists.

Katz, Samuel M. *Raging Within: Ideological Terrorism.* **Minneapolis: Lerner Publications Company, 2003.**
Written by a leading terrorism and counterterrorism expert, this book offers insight into the Shining Path and Túpac Amaru terrorist groups, among others.

Lyle, Garry. *Peru.* **Philadelphia: Chelsea House Publishers, 1999.**
This juvenile-level work looks at Peru's history and geography, with little emphasis on arts and society.

Morrison, Marion. *Peru.* **New York: Children's Press, 2000.**
This standhard text looks at everything from geography to sports and culture in Peru. The book has good pictures and is nicely organized.

Official Site for the Promotion of Peru (Portal del Estado Peruano)
Website: <http://www.perugobierno.gob.pe/frame.asp?dsc_url_web=http%3A// www.peru.org.pe/informacioneng.asp>
Find everything you need to know about Peru at this extensive site. Find information about Peru's history, culture, people, cities, and more.

Parnell, Helga. *Cooking the South American Way.* **Minneapolis: Lerner Publications Company, 2003.**
This title from the Easy Menu Ethnic Cookbooks series features a brief history of South American cuisine, including Peru, as well as tasty recipes from the continent.

Vargas Llosa, Mario. *The Time of the Hero.* **New York: Grove Press, 1966.**
The debut novel of one of the best known Latin American writers, the book is set in the military academy where Vargas Llosa went to school. The work offers insight into Peruvian society.

vgsbooks.com
Website: <http://www.vgsbooks.com>
Visit vgsbooks.com, the home page of the Visual Geography Series®. You can get linked to all sorts of useful on-line information, including geographical, historical, demographic, cultural, and economic websites. The vgsbooks.com site is a great resource for late-breaking news and statistics.

Wilder, Thorton. *The Bridge of San Luis Rey.* **New York: Harper and Row, 1967.**
This classic novel explores fate and life in colonial Peru. It is considered one of the masterpieces of American fiction.

Worth, Richard. *Pizarro and the Conquest of the Inca Empire in World History.* **Berkeley Heights, NJ: Enslow Publishers, Inc., 2000.**
This book examines the conquest of the Incas, a critical turning point in South American history. It looks at Francisco Pizarro and other explorers, as well as the indigenous peoples they conquered.

Captions for photos appearing on cover and chapter openers:

Cover: The city of Machu Picchu sits 8,000 feet (2,438 m) above the Urubamba River valley. Built between 1460 and 1470 by the Inca ruler Pachacuti Inca Yupanqui, the city most likely served as a royal estate and religious retreat.

pp. 4–5 Lake Titicaca is located in southern Peru. Covering 3,200 square miles (8,288 sq. km) and more than 900 feet (274 m) deep in places, it is the largest navigable lake in the world.

pp. 8–9 The Urubamba River valley viewed from Machu Picchu in the Andes Mountains

pp. 20–21 This image of a spider is one of the many drawings of the Nazca Lines. Rediscovered in 1926, the lines are scratched into the desert floor in southern Peru. When viewed from the air, they form geometric patterns and animal drawings. The lines were probably made by the Nazca Indians between 100 B.C. and A.D. 800.

pp. 36–37 Peruvian students pose for the camera at the Plaza de Armas in Cuzco.

pp. 46–47 A Quechua woman burns incense during the Inti Raymi festival at Sacsayhuamán.

pp. 58–59 A young man's boat floats in the harbor of a Peruvian fishing village. Fishing is an important industry in Peru, with more than 4 million tons (3.6 million metric tons) of fish caught each year.

Photo Acknowledgments

The images in this book are used with the permission of: © Michele Burgess, pp. 4–5, 10, 15, 22, 38, 41, 45, 54, 56, 58-59, 61; © Ron Bell/Digital Cartographics, pp. 6, 11; © Robert Fried, pp. 8–9, 36–37, 39, 44, 52; © Layne Kennedy/CORBIS, pp. 12–13; © AFP/CORBIS, p. 14; © Michele Burgess/SuperStock, p. 16; © Carl & Ann Purcell/CORBIS, p. 18; © Yann Arthus-Bertrand/CORBIS, pp. 20–21; Library of Congress, pp. 25 [LC-USZ62-122261], 27 [LC-USZ62-80182]; © Daniel Lainé/CORBIS, p. 26; Image courtesy of Stan Klos, FamousAmericans.net, p. 29; © Bettmann/CORBIS, pp. 31, 32–33; © Reuters NewMedia Inc./CORBIS, pp. 34, 35, 48 (top), 53, 64; © Greg Smith/CORBIS SABA, p. 43; © Nevada Weir, pp. 46–47, 51, 57; © Richard Smith/CORBIS SYGMA, p. 48 (bottom); © Nathan Benn/CORBIS, p. 50; © Bob Krist/CORBIS, p. 62; © Michael S. Yamashita/CORBIS, p. 63; © Todd Strand/Independent Picture Service, p. 68.

Cover: © Robert Fried